Regents English Workbook 2

Intermediate – New Edition

Robert J. Dixson

Prentice Hall Regents
Englewood Cliffs, New Jersey 07632

Library of Congress Cataloging-in-Publication Data

```
Dixson, Robert James.
    Regents English workbook 2 : intermediate / Robert J. Dixson,
  -- New ed.
      p.   cm.
    ISBN 0-13-199101-9 :
    1. English language--Textbooks for foreign speakers.  2. English
  language--Grammar--Problems, exercises, etc.   I.
  II. Title.   III. Title: Regents English Workbook 2.
  PE1128.D523   1995
  428.2'4--dc20                                            94-47009
                                                            CIP
```

Acquisitions Editor: *Nancy Baxer*
Director of Production and Manufacturing: *David Riccardi*
Editorial Production/Design Manager: *Dominick Mosco*
Editorial/Production Supervision and Interior Design: *Dit Mosco*
Cover Art & Design Coordinator: *Merle Krumper*
Cover Design: *Laura C. Ierardi*
Production Coordinator: *Ray Keating*

©1995 by R.J. Dixson Associates
Published by Prentice Hall Regents
Prentice-Hall, Inc.
A Simon & Schuster Company
Englewood Cliffs, New Jersey 07632

Printed in the United States of America
10 9 8 7 6 5

ISBN 0-13-199101-9

Prentice-Hall International (UK) Limited, *London*
Prentice-Hall of Australia Pty. Limited, *Sydney*
Prentice-Hall Canada Inc., *Toronto*
Prentice-Hall Hispanoamericana, S.A., *Mexico*
Prentice-Hall of India Private Limited, *New Delhi*
Prentice-Hall of Japan, Inc., *Tokyo*
Simon & Schuster Asia Pte. Ltd., *Singapore*
Editora Prentice-Hall do Brasil, Ltda., *Rio de Janeiro*

To the Teacher

There is no need here to describe the different types of exercises which this book contains or to discuss their wide variety and extent. A glance through the following pages is enough to acquaint anyone with the book's general contents.

Since this is a workbook, there is also little to say as to how it should be used. Each exercise carries its own instructions, and the students proceed accordingly. On the other hand, there are a few points of general pedagogy which the teacher using the book should keep in mind.

First, this is a workbook, and all explanatory material has been kept to a minimum. Thus, the book is not designed to be used alone or to replace completely the regular classroom text. Rather, this book should be used to supplement the regular classroom text, to give needed variety to the lesson, or to provide additional drill materials on important points of grammar and usage.

Second, as a teacher using this book, don't assume that after students have written the answers to an exercise correctly, they know the material thoroughly and can use the principle in their everyday speech. The exercise is often only the beginning. Much drill and practice are still necessary. Therefore, ask questions or introduce simple conversation involving the particular grammar principle. Also, don't hesitate to repeat the exercises in the book several times. Run over these exercises orally in class. If the students have already written the answers in their books, they can cover these answers with their hand or with a separate sheet of paper. Continue to review past exercises which seem important to you or which have given the students difficulty.

Third, don't fall into the further error of assuming that some of the exercises in this book are too easy for your particular students. Certain exercises may seem easy to you—especially if you speak English as a native—but they still represent a real challenge to anyone studying English as a foreign language. In this connection, there is one additional point of utmost importance which should be kept in mind. We are not interested in these exercises in tricking or even **testing** the student. The exercises are not designed to find out how much a student knows or does not know. Their purpose is simply to drill the student on certain basic points of grammar and usage. The exercises are practice exercises—nothing more. They provide just another means of having students repeat materials which can be learned only through continuous use. For this reason, a good deal of direct repetition has been purposely introduced, not only in individual exercises but throughout the book.

There are three workbooks in the series. Book 1 is for the beginning student; Book 2 is for the intermediate student; Book 3 is for the advanced student. As regards the exact division of material, this plan was followed: The exercises in Book 1 more or less parallel the development by lesson of the material in **Beginning Lessons in English** A and B. Similarly, Book 2 follows the general development of the lessons in **Second Book in English.** Book 3 reviews the material in Books 1 and 2 and focuses on special problems on the advanced level. All the books mentioned are published by Prentice Hall Regents.

Regents English Workbooks are readily adaptable to many uses and can serve effectively to supplement any standard classroom textbook. A perforated answer key at the back of the book makes classroom use or self-study equally feasible.

R.J.D.

Contents

Exercise
Page Number — Structure

1	Review: possessive adjectives
2	Review: object pronouns
3	Review: reflexive pronouns
4	Review: possessive pronouns
5	Review: plural of nouns 1
6	Review: plural of nouns 2
7	Review: third person singular 1
8	Review: third person singular 2
9	Review: simple present tense
10	Review: subject-verb agreement
11	Vocabulary review: opposites 1
12	Prepositions 1
13	Vocabulary review 1
14	General review 1
15	Review: regular verbs, past tense
16	Pronunciation of the past tense
17	Review: irregular verbs, past tense 1
18	Review: irregular verbs, past tense 2
19	Review: negative form 1
20	Review: negative form 2
21	Review: negative form 3
22	Review: question form 1
23	Review: question form 2
24	Review: question form 3
25	*The*
26	Review: present continuous tense
27	Past continuous tense 1
28	Past continuous tense 2
29	Prepositions 2
30	Vocabulary review 2
31	General review 2
32	*Have to:* present tense
33	*Have to:* past, future, and present perfect

Exercise Page Number	Structure
34	*Have to:* negative form
35	*Have to:* question form
36	*Say, tell*
37	Review: present perfect tense
38	Abbreviations
39	Present perfect continuous tense
40	*Since, for, ago*
41	Past perfect tense
42	Review: negative form 4
43	Review: question form 4
44	Prepositions 3
45	Vocabulary review 3
46	Vocabulary review: mistakes of fact 1
47	General review 3
48	Review: contractions
49	Expressions of purpose
50	Review: indirect object position
51	Review: irregular verbs, past participle
52	Future tense with *going to*
53	*Going to:* past tense
54	Sequence of tenses
55	Pronunciation of *s*
56	Pronunciation of *ed* in regular verbs
57	*To get*
58	Silent letters
59	Vocabulary review: mistakes of fact 2
60	Prepositions 4
61	Vocabulary review 4
62	General review 4
63	Passive voice 1
64	Passive voice 2
65	Passive voice 3
66	Passive voice: negative form

Exercise Page Number	Structure
67	Passive voice: question form
68	Review: articles
69	Review: irregular verbs 1
70	Vocabulary review: opposites 2
71	Review: adjectives and adverbs, comparative form
72	*As ... as*
73	Review: *some-any/someone-anyone*
74	Word stress
75	Review: verb tenses
76	Vocabulary review: mistakes of fact 3
77	Prepositions 5
78	Vocabulary review 5
79	General review 5
80	Review: irregular verbs 2
81	*Supposed to*
82	*Used to*
83	Short answers
84	Tag questions 1
85	Tag questions 2
86	Tag questions 3
87	Gerunds 1
88	Gerunds 2
89	Gerunds 3
90	Review: irregular verbs 3
91	Idiomatic expressions
92	Words used as nouns and verbs
93	Corresponding noun and verb forms 1
94	Corresponding noun and verb forms 2
95	Prepositions 6
96	Vocabulary review 6
97	General review 6
98	Questions in indirect speech
99	*Should, ought to*

Exercise Page Number	Structure
100	*Should, ought to:* past form 1
101	*Should, ought to:* past form 2
102	Conditional sentences, future possible 1
103	Conditional sentences, future possible 2
104	Conditional sentences, present unreal 1
105	Conditional sentences, present unreal 2
106	Conditional sentences, present unreal 3
107	Conditional sentences, past unreal 1
108	Conditional sentences, past unreal 2
109	*Wish*
110	Present tense with future clauses
111	Homophones
112	Vocabulary review: opposites from prefixes
113	Prepositions 7
114	Vocabulary review 7
115	General review 7
116	Abbreviated clauses with *too*
117	Abbreviated clauses with *so*
118	Abbreviated clauses with *either* and *neither* 1
119	Abbreviated clauses with *either* and *neither* 2
120	Abbreviated clauses with auxiliary verbs
121	Corresponding noun and adjective forms 1
122	Corresponding noun and adjective forms 2
123	Perfect form of infinitives
124	*Must have, may have*
125	Review: conditional sentences
126	Review: negative form 5
127	Answer Key

1 Review: possessive adjectives

my	our
your	your
his	their
her	
its	
I like *my* new car.	We bought *our* house last year.
She has *her* appointment today.	They drank *their* coffee quickly.

Write the correct pronouns in the blanks.

1. Sylvia usually goes to school with _____ sister.   *her*
2. Frank likes _____ English class very much.   his
3. We spent two hours on _____ homework last night.   our
4. Richard and Nick always do _____ homework
   together.   their
5. Mrs. Teng loves _____ children very much.   her
6. The dog did not eat _____ dinner.   its
7. _____ first name is Anne.   her
8. Do you always do _____ homework in the library?   your
9. I enjoy _____ English class very much.   my
10. Teresa and _____ brother study in the same class.   her
11. We all think a great deal of _____ English teacher.   our
12. Mr. Lee left _____ pen on the desk.   her
13. Yesterday I left _____ notebook on the bus.   _____
14. Most parents love _____ children.   _____
15. Both boys have on _____ new suits.   _____
16. Mariane is wearing _____ new hat today.   _____
17. The cat pays little attention to _____ kittens.   _____
18. Do you always bring _____ lunch to school?   _____
19. Miss Wong left yesterday on _____ vacation.   _____
20. Juan writes a letter to _____ grandparents every
    week.   _____
21. He asked me to help him with _____ shopping.   _____

2 Review: object pronouns

I	me	we	us
you	you	you	you
he	him	they	them
she	her		
it	it		

We use object pronouns as direct objects, indirect objects, and objects of prepositions.

I saw *them* in London.
Roger gave *me* his phone number.
Susan bought the record for *him*.

Change the words in italics to the correct object pronouns.

1. I met *Suzanne* on the street yesterday.   *her*
2. She saw *Noriko and me* in the park. _____
3. She left *her keys* in the car. _____
4. I told *the boys* about it. _____
5. I saw *you and your brother* at the movies last night. _____
6. He rode *his bicycle* to school this morning. _____
7. She told *her parents* about the accident. _____
8. I have *my book* with me. _____
9. We see *those girls* in the park every afternoon. _____
10. I liked *that movie* very much. _____
11. He sent *Nina* some flowers. _____
12. I wrote *your telephone number* in my notebook. _____
13. I eat lunch with *Henry and Charles* every day. _____
14. Put *the cat* outside. _____
15. I don't like to have *animals* in the house. _____
16. I heard *the president* on the radio last night. _____
17. You can go with *Marcia and me* to the party. _____
18. I gave the money to *the maid*. _____
19. Are you going to the movies with *Ali?* _____
20. He put *the money* in the bank. _____
21. She told *her friends* about it. _____

3   Review: reflexive pronouns

myself	ourselves
yourself	yourselves
himself	themselves
herself	
itself	

Reflexive pronouns refer back to the subject of the sentence when the subject and the object are the same person.

Henry hurt *himself* in the game.

Reflexive pronouns emphasize a person or a thing in the sentence.

Lisa *herself* thought of the idea.

We often use the preposition by **and a reflexive pronoun to give the meaning of "alone" or "without help."**

He prefers to do his homework *by himself.* She went to Europe *by herself.*

Write the correct reflexive pronouns in the blanks.

1. Jackie fell and hurt _____.   *herself*
2. I want to buy _____ a new hat.   _____
3. Mr. Oguri _____ will give the principal speech.   _____
4. We _____ will serve the meal.   _____
5. They all enjoyed _____ very much.   _____
6. I also enjoyed _____ very much.   _____
7. The dog hurt _____ when it jumped over the fence.   _____
8. Monique cut _____ with the knife.   _____
9. We need to look at _____ in the mirror.   _____
10. Most children like to look at _____ in the mirror.   _____
11. The president _____ will speak to the members
    of Congress.   _____
12. I _____ will return the book to you.   _____
13. Carlos _____ saw the accident.   _____
14. Mr. Roth arranged the flowers _____.   _____
15. Did you ever cut _____ badly with a knife?   _____
16. He considers _____ too good for the job.   _____
17. I don't like to go to the movies by _____.   _____

mine	ours
yours	yours
his	theirs
hers	
its	

Possessive pronouns are used to avoid repeating the same words in a sentence.

That glass is *my glass.*	That glass is *mine.*
This money is *our money.*	This money is *ours.*

Write the correct possessive pronouns in the blanks.

1. This coat is *her coat.*   *hers*
2. That car is *their car.*   _____
3. This new video is *my new video.*   _____
4. That car stereo is *his car stereo.*   _____
5. That dog in the yard is *our dog.*   _____
6. This desk is *his desk.*   _____
7. Those books are *your books.*   _____
8. This pencil is also *your pencil.*   _____
9. Is this magazine *her magazine?*   _____
10. Your English book is the same as *my English book.*   _____
11. Those books are *Hector and Mario's books.*   _____
12. These books are *my books and your books.*   _____
13. Both these cars are *my cars.*   _____
14. This seat is mine, and the other one is *your seat.*   _____
15. Whose pen is this? Is it *your pen?*   _____
16. Is it *Angela's coat.*   _____
17. I study in my room, and Michel studies in *his room.*   _____
18. I think this notebook is *your notebook.*   _____
19. These pencils are *their pencils.*   _____
20. I found my keys, but Tomiko couldn't find *her keys.*   _____
21. Felipe left *his coat* on the bus.   _____

Most English nouns form the plural by adding s to the singular form.

books	friends	days

Nouns ending in s, sh, ch, x, or z add es to form the plural.

church-churches	kiss-kisses	wish-wishes

Some nouns have irregular plurals.

man-men	foot-feet	mouse-mice	ox-oxen
child-children	tooth-teeth	goose-geese	woman-women

Write the plural form of the following words.

1. lunch   *lunches*
2. tie   _____
3. class   _____
4. teacher   _____
5. beach   _____
6. window   _____
7. door   _____
8. dress   _____
9. watch   _____
10. book   _____
11. ox   _____
12. pencil   _____
13. cafeteria   _____
14. student   _____
15. wish   _____
16. headache   _____
17. box   _____
18. school   _____
19. child   _____
20. tail   _____
21. woman   _____
22. brother   _____

23. notebook   _____
24. hand   _____
25. mouse   _____
26. hat   _____
27. goose   _____
28. loss   _____
29. car   _____
30. cover   _____
31. bus   _____
32. foot   _____
33. dish   _____
34. man   _____
35. kiss   _____
36. face   _____
37. church   _____
38. cousin   _____
39. pen   _____
40. sister   _____
41. match   _____
42. coat   _____
43. cat   _____
44. nose   _____

Nouns ending in y *form their plural in two ways:*

a.	If a vowel precedes the y, add s.
	key–keys toy–toys
b.	If a consonant precedes the y, change the y to i and add es.
	lady–ladies city–cities

Nouns ending in f *or* fe *usually form their plural by changing the endings to* ves.

wife–wives	leaf–leaves	calf–calves

Nouns ending in o, *where* o *is preceded by a consonant, form their plurals by adding* es.

hero–heroes	mosquito–mosquitoes

Write the plural form of the following words.

1.	tomato	*tomatoes*	19.	woman	_____
2.	dish	_____	20.	army	_____
3.	child	_____	21.	half	_____
4.	city	_____	22.	brother	_____
5.	book	_____	23.	leaf	_____
6.	knife	_____	24.	dress	_____
7.	box	_____	25.	sister	_____
8.	potato	_____	26.	match	_____
9.	class	_____	27.	letter	_____
10.	bus	_____	28.	hat	_____
11.	street	_____	29.	man	_____
12.	exercise	_____	30.	lunch	_____
13.	wish	_____	31.	foot	_____
14.	copy	_____	32.	pillow	_____
15.	pen	_____	33.	company	_____
16.	key	_____	34.	lady	_____
17.	church	_____	35.	mouse	_____
18.	hero	_____	36.	wife	_____

Verbs in the third person singular, present tense, follow the general spelling rules for plural nouns.

Most verbs add s.

> he works   she drives

If a verb ends in y **preceded by a consonant, change** y **to** i **and add** es.

> study–he studies   carry–she carries

When a verb ends in o, **we generally add** es.

> go–he goes   do–she does

Verbs ending in s, sh, ch, x, or z **take** es **endings in the third person singular.**

> wish-he wishes   catch-she catches

Change the verb to the third person singular, present tense.

1.	study	*studies*	20.	know	_____
2.	like	_____	21.	think	_____
3.	play	_____	22.	see	_____
4.	go	_____	23.	laugh	_____
5.	carry	_____	24.	match	_____
6.	teach	_____	25.	dance	_____
7.	show	_____	26.	cry	_____
8.	do	_____	27.	pay	_____
9.	watch	_____	28.	sing	_____
10.	try	_____	29.	wish	_____
11.	speak	_____	30.	push	_____
12.	notice	_____	31.	pull	_____
13.	say	_____	32.	dress	_____
14.	pass	_____	33.	miss	_____
15.	wash	_____	34.	use	_____
16.	catch	_____	35.	pass	_____
17.	bring	_____	36.	cash	_____
18.	leave	_____	37.	fix	_____
19.	sit	_____	38.	reply	_____

8 Review: third person singular 2

The auxiliary verbs can, may, must, should, ought, **and** will **do not change spelling in any of the three persons, singular and plural.**

| I *can* go. | You *should* stay. | They *must* leave. |

Change to the third person singular by changing I *to* she. *Write your answers in the blanks at the right.*

1. I know — *She knows*
2. I can speak — *She can speak*
3. I must go — _____
4. I am — _____
5. I have — _____
6. I will see — _____
7. I may study — _____
8. I have seen — _____
9. I am studying — _____
10. I will be — _____
11. I can go — _____
12. I should study — _____
13. I play — _____
14. I carry — _____
15. I go — _____
16. I ought to go — _____
17. I can wait — _____
18. I wait — _____
19. I am waiting — _____
20. I will wait — _____
21. I have waited — _____

22. I like — _____
23. I must see — _____
24. I have been — _____
25. I will take — _____
26. I am working — _____
27. I may work — _____
28. I work — _____
29. I want — _____
30. I do — _____
31. I wish — _____
32. I can meet — _____
33. I try — _____
34. I am leaving — _____
35. I use — _____
36. I wash — _____
37. I am going — _____
38. I will know — _____
39. I must try — _____
40. I have tried — _____
41. I will try — _____
42. I ought to see — _____

9 Review: simple present tense

Write the correct form of the simple present tense of the verbs in parentheses.

1. Yuriko (like) to study English.   *likes*
2. Pauline (have) many friends in this school. _____
3. We (study) in the same class. _____
4. Kenji also (study) in our class. _____
5. He and I (be) good friends. _____
6. Both of our English teachers (be) North Americans. _____
7. They (explain) things very clearly. _____
8. There (be) many students absent today. _____
9. I (watch) television every night. _____
10. My father (listen) to music every night. _____
11. The children (play) in the park every afternoon. _____
12. There (be) someone at the door. _____
13. Juanita (live) on Church Street. _____
14. Alma (go) to the movies almost every night. _____
15. We always (come) to school by bus. _____
16. Peter (do) his homework very carefully. _____
17. He never (make) mistakes in spelling. _____
18. You (be) older than I. _____
19. We both (want) to learn English well. _____
20. They (have) work to do today. _____
21. Nadia (have) two cars. _____
22. She (be) a very rich woman. _____
23. She generally (go) to the United States by plane. _____
24. She sometimes (stay) there for a whole month. _____

subject-verb agreement

Change the italicized words to the plural form. Make the corresponding changes in the verbs. Write only the subject and the verb in your answers.

1. The *book* is on the table.   *The books are* _____
2. *This* is mine.   _____
3. *I* am busy today.   _____
4. *She* likes to study English.   _____
5. *That book* belongs to William.   _____
6. *He* was afraid of the dog.   _____
7. The *boy* does the work well.   _____
8. *He* is writing the exercises.   _____
9. The *child* is afraid of the dog.   _____
10. *This pencil* belongs to Mary.   _____
11. The *tomato* is ripe.   _____
12. The *dish* is on the table.   _____
13. The *class* has started.   _____
14. The *woman* is waiting outside.   _____
15. *This book* is yours.   _____
16. *I* am going to study French.   _____
17. *She* is making good progress.   _____
18. The *bus* is late today.   _____
19. The *man* has left.   _____
20. *He* will leave soon.   _____
21. *She* can speak English well.   _____
22. The *boy* must study more.   _____
23. *She* was here yesterday.   _____
24. The *leaf* is falling from the tree.   _____

opposites 1

Write the opposites of the following words.

1. young	*old*	25. clean	_____
2. high	_____	26. absent	_____
3. arrive	_____	27. beautiful	_____
4. inside	_____	28. happy	_____
5. wild	_____	29. easy	_____
6. awake	_____	30. narrow	_____
7. brave	_____	31. lose	_____
8. hard	_____	32. low	_____
9. sharp	_____	33. under	_____
10. smooth	_____	34. east	_____
11. borrow	_____	35. north	_____
12. forward	_____	36. late	_____
13. polite	_____	37. buy	_____
14. thick	_____	38. tall	_____
15. before	_____	39. often	_____
16. in front of	_____	40. sweet	_____
17. expensive	_____	41. cause	_____
18. dry	_____	42. good	_____
19. false	_____	44. big	_____
21. empty	_____	45. find	_____
22. push	_____	46. remember	_____
23. wide	_____	47. future	_____
24. loose	_____	48. best	_____

Write the correct prepositions in the blanks.

1. I explained the matter _____ her very clearly.   *to*

2. What is the matter _____ him?   _____

3. She seems to be _____ a big hurry.   _____

4. We went there _____ mistake.   _____

5. What has happened _____ Ted?   _____

6. This is an exception _____ the rule.   _____

7. He was absent _____ class twice last week.   _____

8. She should return _____ her book soon.   _____

9. This river is one of the longest _____ the world.   _____

10. They plan to take a trip _____ the world.   _____

11. He says that he'll be back _____ a few minutes.   _____

12. The police officer looked _____ me suspiciously.   _____

13. Angela is looking _____ the book that she lost.   _____

14. How many new words do you look up _____ your
    dictionary every day?   _____

15. They may stay in Europe _____ several months.   _____

16. I plan to go to San Francisco _____ plane.   _____

17. He arrived _____ school twenty minutes late.   _____

18. I do not know the first thing _____ mathematics.   _____

19. She copied her speech word _____ word from the
    encyclopedia.   _____

20. Be sure to write the report _____ the computer.   _____

21. His face is familiar _____ me.   _____

22. Don't mention anything about it _____ him.   _____

23. Let's sit here on this bench _____ a while.   _____

24. She paid _____ credit card.   _____

13 Vocabulary review 1

Select the correct answer and write it in the space provided.

1. The opposite of *generous* is (kind, angry, recent, selfish).   *selfish*

2. A synonym for *recently* is (seldom, never, lately, ultimately). _____

3. We pronounce the word *half* to rhyme with (hall, have, laugh, rough). _____

4. We pronounce the word *sew* to rhyme with (flew, know, cow, blue). _____

5. To *call up* someone is to (criticize, visit, stare at, telephone) him or her. _____

6. To *call on* someone is to (telephone, visit, admire, talk about) him or her. _____

7. To be *about to do* something is to be (interested in doing, at the point of doing, eager to do) it. _____

8. Which of these past tense forms do we pronounce as a word of only one syllable: counted, painted, talked, needed? _____

9. Which letter in the word *wrist* is silent (not pronounced)? _____

10. Which letter in the word *honest* is silent (not pronounced)? _____

11. Which of these words is not spelled correctly: February, excelent, translation, suggestion, convenient? _____

12. What is the corresponding noun form of the adjective *difficult?* _____

13. What is the corresponding noun form of the verb *explain?* _____

14. We pronounce the contraction *she's* to rhyme with (kiss, piece, sneeze, cries). _____

15. The word *possibility* has five syllables. On which syllable do we accent the word—the first, second, third, or fourth syllable? _____

16. If I say that I will be back *by* eight o'clock, this means that I will be back (exactly at eight, about eight, at eight at the latest). _____

14 General review 1

Select the correct form. Write your answers in the blanks.

1. The weather today is warmer (than, as) it was yesterday.   *than*
2. Listen! The water (is running, runs).   _____
3. They (have lived, lived) there since January.   _____
4. We (was, were) both absent from class yesterday.   _____
5. My friend sent (me, to me) a present from Singapore.   _____
6. They (have, are having) their lunch now.   _____
7. There were (many, much) students absent from class this morning.   _____
8. She does not speak English well, (also, either).   _____
9. I didn't hear (someone, anyone) in the room.   _____
10. He (works, has worked) in that company for many years.   _____
11. He always (is coming, comes) to school by bus.   _____
12. I spoke to him (on, by) the telephone yesterday.   _____
13. What time did you (get, got) up this morning?   _____
14. I (wrote, have written) a letter to him yesterday.   _____
15. Rose always (does, makes) many mistakes in spelling.   _____
16. Anne wants (me to go, that I go) with her to the disco tonight.   _____
17. It is not difficult (learn, to learn) English.   _____
18. I don't know where (does he live, he lives).   _____
19. (This, These) pencils belong to Giorgio.   _____
20. He is (a, an) honest man.   _____
21. Sue (has, have) many friends in this school.   _____
22. How many students (is there, are there) in your English class?   _____

regular verbs, past tense

The past tense of regular verbs is formed by adding ed *to their singular form.*

> work–worked   play–played

If the verb ends in e, *only* d *is added.*

> change–changed   close–closed

If the verb ends in y, *preceded by a consonant, change the* y *to* i *and add* ed.

> study–studied   marry–married

If a single final consonant follows a single stressed vowel, double the final consonant before adding ed.

> plan–planned   admit–admitted

Write the past tense form of each of these regular verbs in the blanks at the right.

1.	describe	*described*	18.	enjoy	_____
2.	force	_____	19.	appear	_____
3.	study	_____	20.	help	_____
4.	indicate	_____	21.	travel	_____
5.	need	_____	22.	please	_____
6.	learn	_____	23.	spell	_____
7.	practice	_____	24.	face	_____
8.	use	_____	25.	worry	_____
9.	marry	_____	26.	depend	_____
10.	manage	_____	27.	decrease	_____
11.	carry	_____	28.	remain	_____
12.	play	_____	29.	point	_____
13.	guide	_____	30.	suppose	_____
14.	plan	_____	31.	refer	_____
15.	hope	_____	32.	insist	_____
16.	cry	_____	33.	notice	_____
17.	seem	_____	34.	admit	_____

In regular verbs ending in t **or** d, **the** ed **is pronounced as a separate syllable.**

count–count(ed)	wait–wait(ed)	land–land(ed)

When we add ed **to regular verbs of one syllable not ending in** t **or** d, **they are pronounced as one syllable.**

live-–lived	close–closed	cross–crossed

Pronounce the following past tense forms. Then write the number 1 or 2 to show whether the word is pronounced as a word of one syllable or as a word of two syllables.

1.	ended	**2**	21. rushed	_____
2.	watched	**1**	22. parted	_____
3.	counted	_____	23. cooked	_____
4.	stayed	_____	24. rented	_____
5.	needed	_____	25. lived	_____
6.	called	_____	26. shared	_____
7.	seemed	_____	27. lasted	_____
8.	planned	_____	28. closed	_____
9.	waited	_____	29. helped	_____
10.	washed	_____	30. landed	_____
11.	wanted	_____	31. used	_____
12.	walked	_____	32. hoped	_____
13.	pushed	_____	33. handed	_____
14.	spelled	_____	34. crossed	_____
15.	planted	_____	35. signed	_____
16.	cleaned	_____	36. earned	_____
17.	asked	_____	37. painted	_____
18.	pointed	_____	38. dropped	_____
19.	moved	_____	39. burned	_____
20.	shopped	_____	40. laughed	_____

17 Review: irregular verbs,
past tense 1

Review the forms of the irregular verbs below. Remember that the past tense form is the same as the past participle form for these verbs.

bring	brought	feel	felt	mean	meant
buy	bought	keep	kept	sleep	slept
catch	caught	kneel	knelt	sweep	swept
creep	crept	leave	left	teach	taught
deal	dealt	lose	lost	think	thought

Write the past tense form of the verbs in parentheses. Practice reading these sentences in the past tense.

1. I (sleep) more than ten hours last night.   *slept*
2. He (buy) that car last year.   _____
3. Rob (lose) a hundred dollars at the races yesterday.   _____
4. It was after ten o'clock when she (leave).   _____
5. I didn't understand what he (mean).   _____
6. The police (catch) the thief last night after a long search. _____
7. Sandra (bring) her little brother to class yesterday.   _____
8. They (sweep) each of the rooms carefully.   _____
9. The president's speech (deal) with the subject of taxes.   _____
10. Mike (teach) us English last semester.   _____
11. I (think) I could not come to the lesson today.   _____
12. When Annette won the prize, her family naturally (feel) very proud of her.   _____
13. The dog put his tail between his legs and (creep) out of the room.   _____
14. The teacher asked them to stop, but the two boys (keep) on talking.   _____
15. The little girl (kneel) beside her mother and prayed.   _____
16. Where did you leave your notebook? I (leave) it on the bus.   _____
17. I (mean) to call you yesterday, but I forgot.   _____
18. Although we did not arrive home until late, the cook (keep) the dinner hot for us.   _____
19. Where did you buy your new hat? I (buy) it in London.   _____
20. I (feel) very weak all day yesterday.   _____

past tense 2

Review the forms of the irregular verbs below. Remember that the past tense form is the same as the past participle form. The verbs below form the past tense by changing the vowel sound.

dig	dug	hold	held	shoot	shot
feed	fed	lead	led	sit	sat
fight	fought	meet	met	stand	stood
find	found	read	read	strike	struck
hang	hung	shine	shone	win	won

Hang **has another past tense form,** hanged, **used only in reference to death by hanging.** Shine **also has another past tense form,** shined. **Thus, "The sun** shone**," but "John** shined **his shoes."**

Write the past tense form of the verbs in parentheses. Practice reading these sentences in the past tense.

1. Our team (win) both games last week.   *won*
2. I (find) this book on the bus yesterday.   _____
3. I (meet) him several years ago in Washington.   _____
4. Last year the senior class (hold) its banquet at the
   Springhouse Inn.   _____
5. We (sit) in the first row at the theater last evening.   _____
6. The lightning (strike) two houses in our block last week.   _____
7. Where did you read about the accident? I (read) about it
   in yesterday's newspaper.   _____
8. The police worked on the case for several months before
   they finally (find) the thief.   _____
9. The guide (lead) us down one long hall after another.   _____
10. Dick (hang) up his hat and coat as soon as he came in.   _____
11. Our troops (fight) well, but the enemy was too strong.   _____
12. Where did you hold the meeting? We (hold) it
    in the school auditorium.   _____
13. What did the dog dig up? He (dig) up two old bones.   _____
14. The sun (shine) all day yesterday.   _____
15. They (feed) the guests an excellent meal.   _____
16. We (stand) in line an hour to buy tickets for the show.   _____

The negative of to be, **in both present and past tenses, is formed by placing** not **after the verb.**

> He *is not* a good tennis player.   They *were not* at our party last night.

Form the negative of sentences with auxiliary verbs (can, must, may, will, should, etc.) **by placing** not **after the auxiliary. Remember that** can + not **is spelled as one word.**

> You *should not* break a promise.   We *will not* go by boat this year.

Change the following sentences to the negative form. Include the main verb in your answer where appropriate.

1. Joe will study in our group.   *will not study*
2. You must tell him about it.   _____
3. She may return later.   _____
4. He is very busy today.   _____
5. They were here yesterday.   _____
6. He is studying in our group.   _____
7. She should spend more time on that report.   _____
8. They will be back at five o'clock.   _____
9. She can speak French well.   _____
10. We are going to the movies tonight.   _____
11. They are old friends.   _____
12. She is a good cook.   _____
13. He has gone to Chicago.   _____
14. She will telephone you tonight.   _____
15. We were tired after the dance.   _____
16. I am a computer expert.   _____
17. There is enough sugar in the bowl.   _____
18. There were many students absent last night.   _____
19. I can meet you later.   _____
20. You must type your report on the computer.   _____
21. You may smoke here.   _____

20 Review: negative form 2

The auxiliaries do **and** does + not **are used to form negative sentences in the present tense. Place** do not **or** does not **before the simple form of the verb.**

I speak French well.	She works hard at the office.
I *do not* speak French well.	She *does not* work hard at the office.

To form the negative in the past tense, place did not **before the simple form of the verb.** Did **is used for all persons, singular and plural.**

He came to class early.	We ate a big dinner at noon.
He *did not* come to class early.	We *did not* eat a big dinner at noon.

Change the following sentences to the negative form. Be careful to use the correct auxiliary for the present and past tenses.

1. She comes to class on time.   *does not come*
2. They live near here.   _____
3. I know him very well.   _____
4. I ate two rolls this morning.   _____
5. We want to learn French.   _____
6. The bus stopped on this corner.   _____
7. We cooked dinner at home last night.   _____
8. She sat near me in class.   _____
9. He reads many books in French.   _____
10. He speaks to us in English.   _____
11. Tim smokes too much.   _____
12. She came with me to the lesson.   _____
13. I had a lot of work to do yesterday.   _____
14. The child drank all the milk.   _____
15. Teresa watched television last night.   _____
16. He hung his coat on the chair.   _____
17. I found my book.   _____
18. We sit in the first row at the opera.   _____
19. We learned many new words yesterday.   _____
20. They held the meeting in the school auditorium.   _____
21. The dog dug two holes in the yard.   _____

Change the following sentences to the negative form.
Write the complete verb in the blanks.

1. He will return next week.   *will not return*
2. He speaks English well.   _____
3. It is raining hard.   _____
4. She is a good student.   _____
5. We were late for the lesson this morning.   _____
6. I met Giselle on Fifth Avenue yesterday.   _____
7. Our team won both games.   _____
8. He will be on time this evening.   _____
9. She came to class late this morning.   _____
10. Adela feels much better today.   _____
11. The movie last night was very good.   _____
12. They are going to Spain next year.   _____
13. She can speak English well.   _____
14. You may smoke here.   _____
15. Felipe should spend more time on his homework.   _____
16. They go to the movies every night.   _____
17. I like Italian movies.   _____
18. She is a good teacher.   _____
19. He will tell you the truth.   _____
20. He called on the telephone last night.   _____
21. She is wearing a brown sweater.   _____
22. The train left at four o'clock.   _____
23. I understand him very easily.   _____
24. He speaks very slowly.   _____

22 Review: question form 1

To form questions with to be *in the present and past tenses, place the verb before the subject.*

Is Lisa the best student in your class? *Were your friends* on time yesterday?

Form questions with auxiliaries (can, must, may, will, should, ought, etc.) **by placing the auxiliary before the subject.**

May we leave early today? *Will you* have time to finish before dinner?

Remember that in there + be **sentences,** there **is treated like a subject.**

Change the following sentences to the question form. Write the answer in the space provided.

1. Sam will study in our group. *Will Sam study*
2. She can speak French well. _____
3. She is a politician. _____
4. He may sit here. _____
5. They were tired after the dance. _____
6. She is a good manager. _____
7. He can go with us to the movies. _____
8. He should mention it to her. _____
9. They will be angry. _____
10. She is studying to be a lawyer. _____
11. Mr. Darbari has gone to Chicago. _____
12. She will telephone us later. _____
13. He is an excellent student. _____
14. There were two men in the office. _____
15. He should study more. _____
16. They are old friends. _____
17. They were both here yesterday. _____
18. It is raining hard. _____
19. They are going to a meeting. _____
20. She will be ready soon. _____

Form questions in the simple present tense by placing the auxiliary do **before the subject. Use** does **for the third person singular.**

Do we have enough gas to get home?   *Does Andy* work in your office?

Form questions in the past tense by placing the auxiliary did **before the subject.**

Did Judy drive there by herself?   *Did you* enjoy your holiday in Greece?

Change the following sentences to the question form. Write the auxiliary, followed by the subject and the main verb, in the space provided.

1. She comes to class on time.   *Does she come*
2. They left at two o'clock.   _____
4. He bought a new car last year.   _____
5. She drives her brother to class.   _____
6. Daniela answered the phone.   _____
7. He sat in the first row.   _____
8. He speaks English very clearly.   _____
9. They go to the movies almost every night.   _____
10. They met in Europe last year.   _____
11. The child cut his finger badly.   _____
12. She gave us some good advice.   _____
13. They live on the second floor.   _____
14. You drink milk with your meals.   _____
15. The trolley comes every half hour.   _____
16. The train arrived on time.   _____
17. He writes her every week.   _____
18. They brought Steve a present from New York.   _____
19. He lost his money in Monte Carlo.   _____
20. They caught the thief after a long search.   _____
21. Valentina smokes too much.   _____

Change the following sentences to the question form.
Write the auxiliary, followed by the subject and the main
verb, in the space provided. If the only verb is to be, reverse
the order of the subject and verb.

1. She went to Chicago by plane.   *Did she go* _____
2. He will be in the office on Tuesday. _____
3. Harriet is a good tennis player. _____
4. He works very hard. _____
5. The boys spent the afternoon in the park. _____
6. Paula plays baseball well. _____
7. His sister sings well. _____
8. The telephone is ringing loudly. _____
9. It looks like rain. _____
10. We have enough coffee for everybody. _____
11. The sun is shining now. _____
12. The weather is becoming very warm. _____
13. It rained hard last night. _____
14. Loretta can speak French well. _____
15. He must see a doctor at once. _____
16. Antonia will tell us all about it. _____
17. The man speaks English badly. _____
18. Beatrice could understand him easily. _____
19. The train left on time. _____
20. It will arrive in Philadelphia around noon. _____
21. He has a lot of work to do today. _____
22. She feels better after her operation. _____
23. He wants a better job. _____
24. They spent two weeks in Mexico City. _____

25 The

The *is a definite article. It refers to a particular object or to particular objects.*

| *The* book that I bought is on the table. | *The* pictures you took are excellent. |

Nouns that name an indefinite quantity or an intangible quality do not take an article.

| *Gold* is a precious metal. | *Honesty* is always appreciated. |

When these nouns are used to express a particular quality or quantity, they should be preceded by the.

| *The gold* in this jewelry is very old. | *The honesty* of that child is above question. |

The *is not used before the names of persons, countries, continents, streets, cities, or towns when they are used as proper nouns. (Exceptions:* the United States, *the* Dominican Republic, *etc.)*

| *Ms. Torrence* lives on *White Oak Lane*, in *Fairfax*. She's going to travel to *Europe* next summer. She'll visit *London*, *Paris*, and *Rome*. |

When these words are used as adjectives, they are preceded by the.

| London is a large city. | *The London transportation system* is excellent. |

Write the article the, *if necessary, in the blanks. If it is not necessary, leave blank.*

1. He came here directly from _____ Mexico.   *(no article)*
2. They say that _____ weather in Acapulco is beautiful.   *the*
3. Mr. and Mrs. Bielski are now traveling in _____ Brazil. _____
4. He has always lived in _____ United States. _____
5. Does Maria speak _____ English well? _____
6. _____ English language is not difficult to learn. _____
7. I like _____ tea better than coffee. _____
8. _____ tea in your cup is Japanese. _____
9. _____ women are important in U.S. politics. _____
10. Do you agree that _____ gentlemen speak softly? _____
11. We all took a walk along _____ Fifth Avenue. _____
12. _____ Third Avenue street fair was a big success. _____

26 Review:

present continuous tense

The simple present tense is used to describe an action that happens regularly or in general.

It always *rains* in April here.   They *eat* dinner around eight o'clock.

The present continuous tense describes an action which is occurring at the moment of speaking.

I *am typing* this document. (now)   We *are having* trouble with the computer.

Write the present continuous tense or the simple present tense of the verbs in parentheses.

1. The doorbell (ring) very often.   *rings*
2. The doorbell (ring) now. _____
3. She (write) many letters to her parents. _____
4. Alice is busy now. She (write) a letter. _____
5. Mr. Sato (smoke) too much. _____
6. He (smoke) more than a pack of cigarettes every day. _____
7. Look! He (smoke) a cigarette now. _____
8. It (rain) a great deal during the spring months. _____
9. Look! It (begin) to rain. _____
10. Listen! Someone (knock) at the door. _____
11. The bus always (stop) at this corner. _____
12. The bus (stop) for us now. _____
13. I always (get) on the bus at this corner. _____
14. Mr. and Mrs. Gonzalez (build) a new home on Second Avenue. _____
15. We (have) English lessons three times a week. _____
16. We (have) our English lesson now. _____
17. Look! Rose (wave) to us from across the street. _____
18. Patricia always (come) to school by bus. _____
19. Be quiet or you will wake the baby. She (sleep). _____
20. She (sleep) about fourteen hours a day. _____
21. Mr. Tran (speak) English with a strong foreign accent. _____

Form the past continuous tense with the past tense of to be
and the present participle of the main verb.

I was working	we were working
you were working	you were working
he was working	they were working
she was working	
it was working	

The past continuous is used to describe an action that was going on when another action took place.

I *was sleeping* when you phoned.
We *were leaving* the house when they arrived.

Write the past continuous form of the verbs in parentheses.

1. I (sleep) when you telephoned.   *was sleeping*
2. We (sit) in the park when it began to rain.   _____
3. The sun (shine) brightly when I got up this morning. _____
4. I (walk) down Broadway when I met him.   _____
5. We (have) lunch when she called.   _____
6. Bruce (study) when I went to see him last night.   _____
7. He fell while he (play) in the park.   _____
8. They (drive) to Chicago when the accident happened. _____
9. The teacher (write) on the board when we entered the classroom. _____
10. She fell while she (get) off the bus.   _____
11. My mother (prepare) dinner when I got home.   _____
12. I (have) lunch when I first felt sick.   _____
13. It (rain) hard when I left home.   _____
14. But when I arrived at school, the sun (shine).   _____
15. Molly (talk) with Jack when I passed them in the hall. _____
16. They (watch) television when we called them.   _____
17. I (have) lunch when you telephoned.   _____
18. Both children (sleep) when I went into the room.   _____
19. The man (suffer) greatly when the ambulance arrived. _____

27

Write the correct form of the verb in the simple past or the past continuous tense for each sentence below.

1. I (sleep) well last night.   *slept*
2. I (sleep) when the fire started.   _____
3. When I got up this morning, the wind (blow) hard.   _____
4. It (rain) hard last night.   _____
5. It (rain) hard when I left home.   _____
6. The child fell while she (play) in the park.   _____
7. She (play) in the park all afternoon.   _____
8. We (have) dinner when you telephoned.   _____
9. I (read) two new books last week.   _____
10. When we got there, Keith (read) the newspaper.   _____
11. I (write) several letters last night.   _____
12. I (write) a letter when you called me.   _____
13. The sun (shine) brightly when I got up this morning.   _____
14. The telephone (ring) just as I was leaving.   _____
15. Mr. Ryan (drive) to Chicago in his new car.   _____
16. The accident happened while he (drive) to Chicago.   _____
17. The boys (play) baseball all afternoon yesterday.   _____
18. Pedro fell and hurt himself while he (play) baseball.   _____
19. We (see) Josie at the movie theater last night.   _____
20. We met Yuriko just as she (leave) school.   _____
21. We (wait) an hour for you after class yesterday.   _____
22. While we (wait) for a taxi, Martha came along and took
    us home.   _____

29 Prepositions 2

Write the correct prepositions in the blanks.

1. We arrived _____ Miami at exactly six o'clock.   *in*
2. They live _____ Washington Avenue.   _____
3. He arrived _____ school at nine o'clock.   _____
4. They live across the street _____ us.   _____
5. He listens _____ the radio every night.   _____
6. We stayed _____ the Hotel Roma.   _____
7. She refused to shake hands _____ him.   _____
8. They are going to New York _____ plane.   _____
9. The plane flew directly _____ our house.   _____
10. She placed her coat _____ top of mine.   _____
11. The senator spoke _____ the faculty.   _____
12. There is something wrong _____ this VCR.   _____
13. I spoke to him _____ the telephone last night.   _____
14. I'll call you back _____ twenty minutes.   _____
15. We waited for you _____ an hour.   _____
16. I'll be back _____ ten minutes.   _____
17. They weren't _____ the hotel last night.   _____
18. I am going to Bonnie's house _____ dinner.   _____
19. He is going to ask her _____ a date.   _____
20. What are your plans _____ the weekend?   _____
21. Anne will tell you all _____ our plans.   _____
22. The man died _____ a heart attack.   _____
23. What is the matter _____ John today?   _____
24. He should be more careful _____ his health.   _____
25. She lives far _____ here.   _____

30 Vocabulary review 2

Select the correct answer and write it in the space provided.

1. A person who cannot *hear* is (blind, deaf, sick, busy). **deaf**

2. A person who can read is (smart, legible, literate, oral). _____

3. Which one of these words is not spelled correctly: exhausted, Febuary, Wednesday, participle, anecdote? _____

4. What is the superlative form of the adjective *bad*? _____

5. What is the superlative form of the adjective *good*? _____

6. Which of these verbs is in the past tense: see, go, did, take, bring? _____

7. Which of these auxiliary verbs do we use to form the future tense: do, did, have, will, can? _____

8. Which of these auxiliary verbs do we use to form the present perfect tense: do, did, will, have, can? _____

9. What is the corresponding noun form of the adjective *dangerous*? _____

10. What is the corresponding adjective form of the noun *height*? _____

11. Which of the following words rhymes with *wrist*: fast, least, this, missed? _____

12. Which letter in the words *half, walk*, and *talk* is silent (not pronounced)? _____

13. Which of these animals has a very long neck: tiger, wolf, zebra, giraffe? _____

14. To *call up* someone is to (admire, telephone, visit, study with) him or her. _____

15. To *call off* something is to (tear, need, cancel, postpone) it. _____

16. *Once in a while* means (often, seldom, occasionally, just once). _____

17. Which one of these verbs is an irregular verb: walk, refer, take, want, count? _____

18. Which one of these verbs is a regular verb: see, bring, know, do, pull? _____

19. The opposite of *full* is (big, open, narrow, empty). _____

Select the correct answer and write it in the space provided.

1. They came to class earlier (than, as) we.   *than*

2. She asked me where (I lived, did I live).   _____

3. There (was, were) many students absent from class.   _____

4. He is (a, an) athlete.   _____

5. The last lesson was (a, an) easy one.   _____

6. (This, These) books belong to my brother.   _____

7. The boy (run, ran) from the room.   _____

8. Olga was sick yesterday and (can, could) not come to class.   _____

9. Does Ms. Eng (smoke, smokes) very much?   _____

10. Listen! The stereo (plays, is playing).   _____

11. He has lived in that same house (since, for) many years.   _____

12. I (saw, have seen) that movie last week.   _____

13. When I arrived, they (ate, were eating).   _____

14. Penny always (comes, is coming) to school by bus.   _____

15. He sent (her, to her) a beautiful bouquet of flowers.   _____

16. Look! Isn't that Carmen who (crosses, is crossing) the street?   _____

17. It (rained, was raining) hard when I got up this morning. _____

18. He (works, has worked) for that firm since January.   _____

19. He doesn't know her, and I don't, (also, either).   _____

20. She wants (us to wait, that we wait) for him.   _____

21. We (was, were) all late for the meeting.   _____

22. He says that he has (saw, seen) that movie.   _____

32 *Have to:* present tense

Must **and** have to **express obligation or need. We use**
have to **more often than** must.

You *must* study for this exam.	You *have to* study for this exam.
Harry *must* leave town on business.	Harry *has to* leave town on business.

Change the words in italics to the correct form of have to + *verb.*

1. They *must prepare* their exercises more carefully.   *have to prepare*
2. She *must go* to Chicago tonight.   _____
3. She *must leave* at once.   _____
4. I *must be* there before four o'clock.   _____
5. We *must learn* at least ten new words every day.   _____
6. I *must have* more spending money.   _____
7. Everyone *must work* eight hours a day.   _____
8. He *must go* to the hospital to see his friend.   _____
9. You *must wait* in the reception area.   _____
10. I *must go* to the bank.   _____
11. He *must spend* more time on his homework.   _____
12. I *must go* to the dentist.   _____
13. He *must be* in his office before nine o'clock.   _____
14. We *must leave* before Hugh gets here.   _____
15. You *must write* your answers in the book.   _____
16. Everyone *must write* a composition for tomorrow's lesson.   _____
17. They *must remain* there all afternoon.   _____
18. I *must get* there before three o'clock.   _____
19. She *must remain* in bed for at least three weeks.   _____
20. After that, she *must visit* the doctor every week.   _____

33 *Have to:* past, future, and present perfect

Must *has no past or future tenses. We use* have to *to express obligation or need in the past, future, or present perfect tenses.*

> I *have to* leave early tonight.
> I *had to* leave early last night.
> *I'll have to* leave early tomorrow.
> I *have had to* leave early every day this week.

A. *Change the following sentences to the past tense.*

1. I have to write many letters.   *had to write*
2. He has to leave for school at eight o'clock.   _____
3. She has to work very hard.   _____
4. They have to get up early every morning.   _____
5. We have to walk to school.   _____
6. I have to learn many new words every day.   _____
7. I have to have more money.   _____

B. *Change the following sentences to the future tense.*

1. He has to work very hard.   *will have to work*
2. You have to return later.   _____
3. We have to do this right away.   _____
4. She has to be there before nine o'clock.   _____
5. I have to buy the tickets first.   _____
6. We have to wait at least an hour for him.   _____
7. She has to make an appointment with him.   _____

C. *Change the following sentences to the present perfect tense.*

1. We have to speak clearly.   *have had to speak*
2. Peter has to learn to drive.   _____
3. You have to go on a diet.   _____
4. They have to return from their vacation early.   _____
5. I have to take another flight.   _____
6. Angela has to cook for twenty guests.   _____
7. You have to buy new shoes.   _____

34 *Have to:* negative form

To form the negative with have to, **place** do not, does not, did not, **or** will not **before** have. **The contracted forms** don't, doesn't, didn't, **and** won't **are normally used.**

I *have to* catch the seven-thirty train.	I *don't have to* catch the seven-thirty train.
Lisa *will have to* stay with you.	Lisa *won't have to* stay with you.
They *had to* help me.	They *didn't have to* help me.

Change the following sentences to the negative form. Use contractions.

1. She has to work late tonight.   *doesn't have to work*
2. He had to leave early. _____
3. We have to study hard for our next exam. _____
4. I have to write that letter at once. _____
5. I had to wait a long time to see him. _____
6. She has to spend more time on her homework. _____
7. I have to return later. _____
8. He has to be at his office before eight o'clock. _____
9. They have to leave before Wednesday. _____
10. We had to walk to school. _____
11. You will have to send him a telegram. _____
12. You have to wait for me. _____
13. We had to pay the doctor for her services. _____
14. I had to go to the bank. _____
15. I have to cash his check today. _____
16. We will have to invite Mary to the party. _____
17. She has to take an exam in English. _____
18. He had to join the navy. _____
19. She has to leave for Mexico this week. _____
20. We have to write a composition every week. _____
21. We had to write a letter to the lawyer. _____

35   *Have to:* question form

To form questions with have to, **place** do, does, did, **or** will **before the subject.**

Sally *has to* play in a tennis match.	Does Sally *have to* play in a tennis match?
We *will have to* be ready early.	*Will* we *have to* be ready early?

Change the following sentences to the question form.

1. John has to stay home tonight.   *Does John have to stay*

2. He had to stay home last night, too.   _____

3. The students have to learn many new words.   _____

4. They will have to write a composition each week.   _____

5. She had to wait for him for an hour.   _____

6. You have to return later.   _____

7. She had to go to the doctor.   _____

8. She has to take another exam.   _____

9. We had to invite Eric to the party.   _____

10. He has to leave for Europe next week.   _____

11. We will have to write our exercises carefully.   _____

12. They have to arrive at school before nine o'clock.   _____

13. Tom has to get up early every morning.   _____

14. Sue has to help her mother.   _____

15. She had to prepare the dinner.   _____

16. She has to work very hard.   _____

17. They had to stay home last night and study.   _____

18. He has to go to the hospital for an operation.   _____

19. I have to sign my name at the bottom of the page.   _____

20. We had to send him a telegram.   _____

21. We have to save every cent possible.   _____

36 Say, tell

Say *is used in direct quotations.*

> Joseph *said,* "It's too early to leave for the theater."
> She *said* to me, "Your computer print-out is ready."

Say *is used for indirect quotations where the person to whom the words are spoken is not mentioned.*

> Harvey *said* that he could not come tomorrow.

Tell *is used for indirect quotations when the person to whom the words are spoken is mentioned.*

> Harvey *told me* that he could not come tomorrow.

Tell *is used in the following expressions: to tell the truth, to tell a lie, to tell a story, to tell time, to tell a secret, to tell about something.*

The word that, *when used to introduce a subordinate clause as in these sentences, is often dropped in everyday speech. We may say, "She said that she was busy" or "She said she was busy." Both forms are correct.*

Write the correct form of say *or* tell *in the blanks.*

1. She _____ both of us (that) she was going to get married.   *told*
2. Roger _____ (that) he was busy after class.   _____
3. He _____ (that) he always ate lunch in the cafeteria.   _____
4. Sally _____ (that) it was the truth.   _____
5. I _____ you (that) the car belonged to George.   _____
6. Martin _____ him (that) the house was for sale.   _____
7. Susan _____ (that) she could teach me to paint.   _____
8. Robert _____, "The book is from the library."   _____
9. Can you _____ me where Ms. Nomura's office is?   _____
10. He _____ (that) he understood Polish.   _____
11. Dolores _____ (that) she felt ill.   _____
12. I _____ the teacher (that) I already knew how to type.   _____
13. He _____ me (that) Marc was in the hospital.   _____
14. Annette _____ us (that) it was a good hotel.   _____

36

I have worked	we have worked
you have worked	you have worked
he has worked	they have worked
she has worked	
it has worked	

The present perfect tense is for an action that began in the past and is still continuing.

> She *has owned* her house since 1984. (She still owns it.)
> We *have known* Bill for years. (We know him now.)

Remember that the simple past tense describes an action which happened at a definite time in the past.

> We *went* there last year.

Write the simple past tense or present perfect tense of the verbs in parentheses.

1. We live on 72nd Street, where we (live) for almost five years. _____ *have lived*
2. From 1975 to 1980, we (live) on 96th Street. _____
3. Marie-France (begin) to study English as soon as she arrived in the United States. _____
4. She (study) English continuously since then. _____
5. Ricardo (study) French when he was in high school. _____
6. The First World War (begin) in 1914 and ended in 1918. _____
7. It (last) for four years. _____
8. We (be) in California last winter. _____
9. They (live) in California since 1974. _____
10. My last car was a Chevrolet. I (have) it for four years. _____
11. My present car is a Buick. I (have) it for two years. _____
12. Sonia and I are good friends. In fact, we (be) good friends for more than ten years. _____
13. We (become) friends when we were students in the university. _____
14. Dr. Pavlik (be) our family doctor ever since we moved to this town. _____

38 Abbreviations

Write the full form of the items which appear below.

1.	6 oz.	*six ounces*	25.	4 ft.	_____
2.	1 lb.	_____	26.	96th St.	_____
3.	1 mi.	_____	27.	Ave.	_____
4.	7 a.m.	_____	28.	Blvd.	_____
5.	6 p.m.	_____	29.	Rd.	_____
6.	.6	_____	30.	Bldg.	_____
7.	1/2	_____	31.	Feb.	_____
8.	1/4	_____	32.	Aug.	_____
9.	6%	_____	33.	Dec.	_____
10.	#5	_____	34.	sq. ft.	_____
11.	68°	_____	35.	1st	_____
12.	AC	_____	36.	3rd	_____
13.	DC	_____	37.	7th	_____
14.	etc.	_____	38.	Thurs.	_____
15.	1 gal.	_____	39.	Wed.	_____
16.	TV	_____	40.	NBC	_____
17.	C.O.D.	_____	41.	NY	_____
18.	qt.	_____	42.	CA	_____
19.	pt.	_____	43.	IL	_____
20.	yd.	_____	44.	WA	_____
21.	in.	_____	45.	CT	_____
22.	&	_____	46.	OH	_____
23.	Inc.	_____	47.	MI	_____
24.	2 yrs.	_____	48.	TN	_____

tense

The present perfect continuous tense is formed with
have/has been **and the present participle of the main verb.**

I have been working	we have been working
you have been working	you have been working
he has been working	they have been working
she has been working	
it has been working	

The present perfect continuous tense is used to describe an action that began in the past and is continuing in the present.

> We *have been living* here for eight years.
> Bruce *has been studying* law since last year.

Write the present perfect continuous tense of the verbs in parentheses.

1. She (study) English for two years.   *has been studying*
2. We (live) in this house since last March.   _____
3. I (try) to reach you by phone for the last hour.   _____
4. He (drive) that same old car for at least ten years.   _____
5. She (feel) much better recently.   _____
6. He (sit) on that bench for several hours.   _____
7. Rose (work) on that same problem for several days.   _____
8. They (talk) on the telephone for over an hour.   _____
9. She naturally speaks English well because she (speak) it all her life.   _____
10. He (work) in that same office ever since I first met him.   _____
11. Ms. Russo (teach) school for many years.   _____
12. They (go) together for almost a year.   _____
13. I (wait) here for you for almost an hour.   _____
14. It (rain) all day long.   _____
15. You (whistle) that same tune for the last hour.   _____
16. She (study) music since she was a child.   _____
17. She (wear) that same hat for more than a year.   _____
18. They (work) there for a long time.   _____
19. We (plan) this trip for many months.   _____

40 Since, for, ago

For **shows the length of time of the action in the present, past, and future tenses.**

> We have lived here *for* six years.   She'll stay in Europe *for* a year.

Since **tells when the action began.**

> They have lived here *since* 1978.

Ago **refers to how much time back in the past something happened.**

> My ancestors arrived in this country 175 years *ago*.

Write since, for, or ago *in the blanks.*

1. I met him on the street about two weeks _____.   *ago*
2. He has been studying English _____ last January.   _____
3. She has been studying English _____ two years.   _____
4. I visited them in Miami about six months _____.   _____
5. He stayed with us _____ about six months.   _____
6. Clara has lived in that same house _____ many years.   _____
7. They have lived there _____ 1984.   _____
8. She has never been the same _____ he went away.   _____
9. He has been sick _____ several days.   _____
10. She has been sick _____ Wednesday.   _____
11. How long _____ did the accident happen?   _____
12. I haven't seen Chris _____ last Christmas.   _____
13. We talked _____ about two hours.   _____
14. She has been in the hospital _____ July.   _____
15. He left for Chicago three days _____.   _____
16. I haven't talked with her _____ yesterday.   _____
17. I talked with her _____ a few minutes yesterday.   _____
18. Mr. Pelli has been teaching English ever _____ he returned to the United States.   _____
19. She first began to teach English about three years _____.   _____
20. She has been teaching English _____ many years.   _____

41 Past perfect tense

To form the past perfect tense, use had *and the past participle of the main verb.*

I had finished	we had finished
you had finished	you had finished
he had finished	they had finished
she had finished	
it had finished	

The past perfect tense is used to tell about an action which began and ended in the past before another past action. It is used with the past tense, either stated or implied.

> By the time you arrived, they *had* already *left*.
> It *had burned* down before the first fire trucks arrived.

Write the past perfect tense of the verbs in parentheses.

1. He told me that he (visit) Miami several times. *had visited*
2. I thought it was the stranger who (steal) the money. _____
3. I saw that we (take) the wrong road. _____
4. She said that she (have) her lunch. _____
5. I thought he (find) his keys. _____
6. I told him that I (see) the movie. _____
7. When we arrived, they already (leave). _____
8. I visited many of the places where I (play) as a boy. _____
9. We got there just ten minutes after he (leave). _____
10. She (live) there two years when the war began. _____
11. He said that he (look) everywhere for it. _____
12. She told us that she already (take) the money to the bank. _____
13. I was sure that he (have) the same trouble before. _____
14. The police said that they (receive) several similar reports the same evening. _____
15. What did he say he (do) with the money? _____
16. He said that he (put) it back where he had found it. _____
17. By the time we got there, all the other guests (leave). _____
18. We saw, as soon as we arrived home, that someone (break) into the house. _____

42 Review: negative form 4

Change the following sentences to the negative form.

1. He knows English well.   *does not know*
2. She left yesterday for California. _____
3. Anne is a very good student. _____
4. I wanted to take a walk. _____
5. He has studied English for many years. _____
6. He told her all about his plans. _____
7. They will return on Wednesday. _____
8. He is having his lunch now. _____
9. They have left for the station. _____
10. She can speak French well. _____
11. You must tell him about it. _____
12. They are going to the movies with us. _____
13. It is a beautiful day. _____
14. It was a very pleasant day. _____
15. She has worked in that office for many years. _____
16. They have been living there for a long time. _____
17. She has to work tonight. _____
18. She had to go to the hospital to see a friend. _____
19. He came to the lesson yesterday. _____
20. They are making good progress in their studies. _____
21. He told me to wait for him. _____
22. She prepares her lessons carefully. _____
23. They were playing tennis at the time. _____
24. Julia has finished that work. _____

43 Review: question form 4

Change the following sentences to the question form.

1. She works on the tenth floor.   *Does she work*
2. He gave her the message.   _____
3. She is a good friend of hers.   _____
4. We are going to the movies tonight.   _____
5. They will return home on Wednesday.   _____
6. He left his keys at home.   _____
7. Marcia can swim very well.   _____
8. She is going to study French next year.   _____
9. He has read that novel before.   _____
10. She has been studying English for many years.   _____
11. She is very eager to learn English well.   _____
12. We have to have more practice in conversation.   _____
13. Robert had to leave for New York yesterday.   _____
14. He will return in a few days.   _____
15. They were having lunch at the time.   _____
16. They built that bridge last year.   _____
17. They will deliver the merchandise tomorrow.   _____
18. She was here at three o'clock.   _____
19. It is almost three o'clock.   _____
20. The wind is blowing very hard.   _____
21. There were many people in the park.   _____
22. The child cut herself badly.   _____
23. The boy ran between the two cars.   _____
24. The doorbell is ringing now.   _____

Write the correct prepositions or particles in the blanks.

1. The exercise was too difficult _____ him to do.   *for*
2. It was kind _____ you do that for her.   _____
3. She is worried _____ her husband's health.   _____
4. They are putting _____ several new buildings in
   that block.   _____
5. The bus doesn't stop _____ this corner.   _____
6. Have you heard _____ Sally's new baby?   _____
7. Nora wants to go _____ a diet.   _____
8. What are they laughing _____?   _____
9. What was he talking _____?   _____
10. He has been studying English _____ three years.   _____
11. She has worked in that office _____ last year.   _____
12. We hung the pictures _____ the fireplace.   _____
13. The temperature dropped from ten degrees above
    zero to ten degrees _____ zero.   _____
14. Why don't you sit _____ a more comfortable chair?   _____
15. That building seems to be _____ fire.   _____
16. The elevator is not running today. It is _____ of order. _____
17. What is the matter _____ him?   _____
18. I make many mistakes _____ spelling.   _____
19. I see Josie in the cafeteria _____ time to time.   _____
20. I will get _____ touch with you next week.   _____
21. He seems to be _____ a hurry.   _____
22. She was absent _____ class twice last week.   _____
23. He came to school _____ spite of the fact that he
    was not feeling well.   _____
24. This book belongs _____ Nancy.   _____

Select the correct answer and write it in the space provided.

1. The opposite of *sharp* is (new, funny, dull, necessary).   *dull*

2. *I'd rather go* means that I (want to, prefer to, had better, seldom) go. _____

3. Which of these words is not spelled correctly: breakfast, secretary, committee, entrence? _____

4. What is the corresponding noun form of the verb *to agree?* _____

5. What is the corresponding verb form of the noun *explosion?* _____

6. Which one of these verbs has the same form in the past tense as in the present tense: go, walk, take, put, see? _____

7. Which of these is a past participle: find, thank, saw, been, went? _____

8. We pronounce the word *comb* to rhyme with (come, sum, tomb, home). _____

9. We pronounce the word *axe* to rhyme with (fix, fast, lacks, first). _____

10. If a man does something *by himself,* he does it (well, hurriedly, to himself, alone). _____

11. A synonym for *besides* is (alongside, near, in addition to, close). _____

12. What is the corresponding noun form of the verb *to advise?* _____

13. The opposite of *frequently* is (often, new, seldom, now). _____

14. *Lately* means (often, very soon, recently, later). _____

15. *I'm kidding* means I'm (smiling, joking, crying, laughing). _____

16. Which letter in the word *answer* is silent (not pronounced)? _____

17. Which letter in the word *listen* is silent (not pronounced)? _____

mistakes of fact 1

The items in boldface are mistakes. Change them to make the facts correct, and write your answers in the blanks.

1. There are **thirteen** months in a year.   *twelve*

2. The capital of the United States is **Philadelphia**.   _____

3. Ten divided by two is **four**.   _____

4. We pronounce the word *talked* as a word of
   two syllables.   _____

5. Tigers and lions are **domestic** animals.   _____

6. We use the indefinite article *an* before words which
   begin with a **consonant**.   _____

7. We accent the word *television* on the **fourth** syllable. _____

8. We call those verbs which form their past tense
   by adding *ed* to the present tense **irregular** verbs.   _____

9. The next to the last month of the year is **October**.   _____

10. The sun always **sets** in the east.   _____

11. There are **four** pints in a quart.   _____

12. There are **eighteen** ounces in a pound.   _____

13. In the United States, we always celebrate
    Thanksgiving Day on a **Tuesday**.   _____

14. Canada lies **east** of the United States.   _____

15. The auxiliary verb which we use in English to form the
    present perfect tense is **will**.   _____

16. The coldest season of the year in the United States is
    autumn.   _____

17. There are **fifty-six** weeks in a year.   _____

18. The verb *take* is the kind of verb called **regular**.   _____

19. The past participle of *take* is **took**.   _____

20. The English alphabet has **twenty-four** letters.   _____

21. On a watch or clock, the minute hand is **shorter**
    than the hour hand.   _____

22. Abraham Lincoln was president of the United States
    during the **Revolutionary War**.   _____

Select the correct form. Write your answers in the blanks.

1. Marie has worked in that office (for, since) many years. *for*
2. Tony said that he (saw, had seen) that movie. _____
3. When we arrived, Alice (read, was reading) the newspaper. _____
4. This book is mine, and that one is (your, yours). _____
5. We (must, had to) go to the hospital last night to see a friend who is sick. _____
6. We (haven't to, don't have to) work tomorrow because it is a holiday. _____
7. We (have been, were) in California for two months last winter. _____
8. I saw that we (take, were taking) the wrong road. _____
9. I said that we (needed, were needing) a map. _____
10. What time did you (leave, left) home this morning? _____
11. Hurry! The bus (comes, is coming). _____
12. They (have, are having) their dinner now. _____
13. The teacher explained (us, to us) the meaning of the word. _____
14. Rita wants (me to go, that I go) to the movies with her. _____
15. He gave (me, to me) all the money he had. _____
16. The wind (is blowing, blows) very hard during the month of March. _____
17. I didn't hear (someone, anyone) in the next room. _____
18. We (went, have gone) to the movies last night. _____
19. We (are, have been) friends for many years. _____
20. Julio (said, told) that he could not come to the party. _____
21. Listen! The birds (sing, are singing). _____
22. He is (a, an) old friend of hers. _____

To be

I'm	we're
you're	you're
he's	they're
she's	
it's	

Certain auxiliaries are also commonly used in the contracted form:
I'll (I will), I've (I have), you've (you have), she'd (she had), etc.

Remember that we usually use the contracted form with negatives and auxiliary verbs.

isn't, wasn't, won't, can't, don't, didn't, haven't, etc.

Change the words in italics to the contracted form.

1. *I am* very busy today.   *I'm*
2. *You are* a good friend of his.   _____
3. *She is* going to the movies with us.   _____
4. *It is* raining.   _____
5. *She is* the best student in the class.   _____
6. *We are* very old friends.   _____
7. *They are* having their lunch now.   _____
8. *There is* someone in the next room.   _____
9. *You are* here too early.   _____
10. *I will* meet you at six o'clock.   _____
11. *You will* be late if you don't hurry.   _____
12. *She will* return next week.   _____
13. *We will* be back at five o'clock.   _____
14. I *do not* know her well.   _____
15. He *does not* speak English.   _____
16. They *did not* come to the meeting last night.   _____
17. I *will not* be able to meet you tomorrow.   _____
18. Nancy *will not* return until Wednesday.   _____
19. They *are not* going to the movies with us.   _____
20. I *have not* seen that movie.   _____

49 Expressions of purpose

Use in order to **or** to **followed by the simple form of the verb to express purpose. The short form** (to) **is more common in everyday conversation.**

We went to the hospital *in order to* see our friend.
We went to the hospital *to* see our friend.

For **is used before nouns to express purpose.**

I went to the store *for* some ice cream.
She's shopping *for* a new stereo.

Use to *or* for *to complete the following sentences.*

1. She went to town _____ buy some gas.   *to*

2. She has gone to the corner store _____ some vegetables.   _____

3. He went to the bank _____ some money.   _____

4. He went to the bank _____ get some money.   _____

5. He is going to go to Florida _____ his health.   _____

6. Barbara came _____ the books that you promised to lend her.   _____

7. I have to go to the post office _____ mail a letter.   _____

8. He first came to this country _____ visit his relatives.   _____

9. I'll stop at the theater _____ the tickets that you bought.   _____

10. I'll stop at the theater _____ pick up the tickets that you bought. _____

11. We are going to the airport _____ meet some friends.   _____

12. Martha is coming to our house tonight _____ dinner.   _____

13. He is coming to the United States just _____ study English.   _____

14. Some friends came _____ visit us last night.   _____

15. He often waits after class just _____ talk with the teacher.   _____

16. She went to the florist's _____ buy some flowers.   _____

**If the indirect object follows the direct object, the preposition
to or for is used. If the indirect object precedes the direct object,
we do not use a preposition.**

He handed the phone *to me*.	He handed *me* the phone.
I bought a new tennis racquet *for* Ruth.	I bought *Ruth* a new tennis racquet.

Some verbs that function this way are give, send, bring, tell, write, **and** buy.

*Change the following sentences so that the indirect object comes
before the direct object. Write only the main verb and the indirect
object in the spaces provided.*

1. He gave the money to her.   *gave her*
2. I gave the tickets to Antonia.   _____
3. I sent some money to him for his birthday.   _____
4. Don't show these things to Rudy.   _____
5. She paid the money to the landlord.   _____
6. He sold the books to his friend.   _____
7. I took the flowers to her.   _____
8. She brought a box of candy to me.   _____
9. He bought a new car for his wife.   _____
10. She brought many presents to us from abroad.   _____
11. I will write a letter to you next week.   _____
12. She gave the money to her father to put in the bank.   _____
13. We sent some flowers to Ms. Pappas.   _____
14. I told the whole story to Sharon.   _____
15. He gave a piece of the candy to each of us.   _____
16. He lent a large sum of money to his brother.   _____
17. Please hand those plates to me.   _____
18. She sent a postcard to each of them.   _____
19. The teacher gave a good mark to Mike.   _____
20. They will send the merchandise to us next week.   _____
21. He lent his car to us for the afternoon.   _____
22. She may bring a present for me from Bali.   _____

past participle

Study and memorize the following list of irregular verbs. This list shows many of the verbs that end in an n sound in the past participle form.

bite	bit	bitten	eat	ate	eaten
blow	blew	blown	fall	fell	fallen
break	broke	broken	fly	flew	flown
choose	chose	chosen	freeze	froze	frozen
do	did	done	get	got	gotten
draw	drew	drawn	give	gave	given
drive	drove	driven	go	went	gone

Write the correct form of the verbs in the sentences below.

1. Yesterday the wind (blow) down the tree in front of our house.   *blew*
2. All the birds have (fly) south for the winter.   _____
3. He told us that he had (drive) the car more than a hundred thousand miles.   _____
4. Last night thieves (break) into our neighbor's home.   _____
5. It is the third time that someone has (break) into her home.   _____
6. While he was skating in the park yesterday, Alex (fall) and hurt himself.   _____
7. He has (fall) many times before but never hurt himself.   _____
8. We (do) some exercises similar to these last week.   _____
9. I went to the bank this morning and (draw) out all my money.   _____
10. Someone told me that Alice has (go) back to California for good.   _____
11. We (eat) lunch in the school cafeteria yesterday.   _____
12. It was so cold last winter in Europe that more than a hundred people (freeze) to death.   _____
13. I met Tom yesterday and (give) him the money that I owed him.   _____
14. At the meeting last night, we (choose) Nina as the new president of our club.   _____
15. That dog has (bite) several people.   _____
16. Have you (do) your homework yet?   _____

52 Future tense with *going to*

In addition to will + *the simple form of the verb to express the future tense, we form the future tense with the appropriate form of* to be going to *and the simple form of the verb. The contracted forms are normally used.*

I *am going to* see	(*I'm going to* see)	we *are going to* see
you *are going to* see	(*you're going to* see)	(*we're going to* see)
he *is going to* see	(*he's going to* see)	you *are going to* see
she *is going to* see	(*she's going to* see)	(*you're going to* see)
it is going to see	(it's going to see)	they are going to see
		(*they're going to* see)

We generally shorten such sentences as "He is going to go **to Mexico on his vacation" to "He** is going **to Mexico on his vacation."**

Write the correct form of the verbs in the sentences below.

1. He (wait) for us after the lesson.   *is going to wait*
2. Michel (teach) me how to swim.   _____
3. Hurry! We (be) late for the lesson.   _____
4. She (meet) us after the theater.   _____
5. We (stay) home and watch television tonight.   _____
6. He (go) to Mexico on his vacation.   _____
7. She (take) engineering in college.   _____
8. We (go) to the beach this afternoon.   _____
9. The paper says that it (rain) tomorrow.   _____
10. We (eat) out tonight.   _____
11. Martin (have) dinner with us.   _____
12. After dinner we (go) to the theater.   _____
13. She (get) married in June.   _____
14. They (spend) their honeymoon in Bermuda.   _____
15. Tom (ask) Juanita for a date.   _____
16. You (be) late for class if you don't hurry.   _____
17. We (go) to the movies tonight.   _____
18. They (fly) to Rangoon.   _____
19. He (study) English by himself.   _____

53 *Going to:* past tense

The past form of going to *indicates an action that was planned but did not happen. To form the past tense, use the correct past tense form of* to be going to *and the simple form of the verb.*

I was going to move	we were going to move
you were going to move	you were going to move
he was going to move	they were going to move
she was going to move	
it was going to move	

We generally shorten such sentences as "I was going to go **shopping this afternoon" to "I** was going **shopping this afternoon."**

Write the correct form of the paste tense of to be going to *and the simple form of the verb. Use the long form of* to be going to go.

1. We (play) bridge last night, but our guests never arrived.
   were going to play

2. I (go) shopping this afternoon, but I had too much work to do at home.
   _____

3. She (study) abroad last year but finally changed her plans.
   _____

4. We (go) to the beach yesterday, but it rained too hard.
   _____

5. I (call) you last night, but I was too busy.
   _____

6. He (see) a doctor about the pain in his back, but suddenly the pain disappeared.
   _____

7. We (buy) a new television set but decided to wait until next year.
   _____

8. They (visit) us last night but later changed their plans.
   _____

9. He always said that he (be) a doctor when he grew up, but he finally went into business.
   _____

10. We (eat) out last night, but the weather was too bad. _____

11. I (send) him a telegram but later decided to telephone.
    _____

12. She (lend) me the money, but her husband was opposed to it.
    _____

13. He (let) me know when he arrived, but he failed to do so.
    _____

When the main verb of the sentence is in the past tense, all dependent verbs are generally in the past tense, too.

Jerry *says* he *will* come to the party.	Jerry *said* he *would* come to the party.
I *know* this test *will* be difficult.	I *knew* this test *would* be difficult see)

Note the irregular past tense form of the following auxiliary verbs:

will	would
can	could
may	might
have	had

Choose the correct word to complete the following sentences.

1. Sarah said that she (will, would) be late for the lesson.   *would*
2. I thought it (is, was) going to rain. _____
3. He didn't think he (can, could) go with us. _____
4. The newspaper said that the weather today (will, would) be cold. _____
5. He said that his first name (is, was) Robert. _____
6. I asked him where he (lives, lived). _____
7. She said her name (is, was) Brigitte. _____
8. I asked him whether he (likes, liked) New Delhi. _____
9. The man told me that he (lives, lived) in Mexico. _____
10. He also said that he (can, could) speak Spanish well. _____
11. I thought I (will, would) be late for the lesson. _____
12. She said she (may, might) go with us to the movies tonight. _____
13. I didn't know what his last name (is, was). _____
14. She told me she (has lost, had lost) her pocketbook. _____
15. She explained to me what the word (means, meant). _____
16. I asked the boy how old he (is, was). _____
17. He told me that he (will, would) help me with the work. _____
18. I thought I (may, might) be too late to see her. _____
19. I saw at once that he (is, was) a serious student. _____
20. I asked him what time it (is, was). _____

The letter s **is pronounced** s **in words such as** pass, this, see, **and** ask. **The letter** s **is pronounced** z **in words such as** his, does, rose, **and** goes.

Practice listening to and pronouncing the different s sounds. Write s or z or show how the letter is pronounced.

1.	easy	*z*	23.	this	_____
2.	pass	*s*	24.	these	_____
3.	mouse	_____	25.	those	_____
4.	bus	_____	26.	kiss	_____
5.	news	_____	27.	his	_____
6.	raise	_____	28.	goes	_____
7.	seat	_____	29.	some	_____
8.	does	_____	30.	first	_____
9.	comes	_____	31.	cousin	_____
10.	eats	_____	32.	tries	_____
11.	rose	_____	33.	brings	_____
12.	class	_____	34.	likes	_____
13.	bus	_____	35.	puts	_____
14.	peas	_____	36.	dogs	_____
15.	tennis	_____	37.	cats	_____
16.	knows	_____	38.	was	_____
17.	nose	_____	39.	case	_____
18.	books	_____	40.	movies	_____
19.	eyes	_____	41.	plays	_____
20.	pens	_____	42.	tries	_____
21.	dress	_____	43.	cost	_____
22.	closed	_____	44.	is	_____

in regular verbs

The final ed *in the past tense of regular verbs takes two different pronunciations:*

> a. When ed is added to a verb ending in an unvoiced consonant (p, t, f, k, s, etc.), the final d is pronounced t.
>
> b. When ed is added to a verb ending in a voiced consonant (b, d, v, g, z, l, etc.), or in a vowel sound, the final d is pronounced d.

Write t or d to show the pronunciation of the ed in each word.

1.	lived	*d*	22.	boiled	_____
2.	picked	*t*	23.	finished	_____
3.	jumped	_____	24.	burned	_____
4.	placed	_____	25.	filled	_____
5.	hurried	_____	26.	passed	_____
6.	rushed	_____	27.	excused	_____
7.	smoked	_____	28.	mailed	_____
8.	killed	_____	29.	slipped	_____
9.	looked	_____	30.	liked	_____
10.	dropped	_____	31.	used	_____
11.	turned	_____	32.	changed	_____
12.	crossed	_____	33.	worked	_____
13.	entered	_____	34.	studied	_____
14.	stopped	_____	35.	talked	_____
15.	earned	_____	36.	spelled	_____
16.	knocked	_____	37.	thanked	_____
17.	saved	_____	38.	washed	_____
18.	played	_____	39.	poured	_____
19.	wished	_____	40.	walked	_____
20.	showed	_____	41.	pulled	_____
21.	closed	_____	42.	tried	_____

Idiomatic Meanings:

To get (someplace) means "to arrive."

I *got* home late last night.	Her flight *gets* here at ten P.M.

To get means "to buy."

He *got* a new suit on sale.	We're *getting* a word processor for the office.

To get, with various adjectives, means "to become."

Gabriela *got* angry when you said that.	I always *get* hungry at this time of day.

To get is used in many idiomatic expressions, for example, to get up, to get on, to get in, to get over.

In the following sentences, substitute the proper phrase with a form of to get *for the words in italics.*

1. He *became angry* with us because we left so early.   *got angry*
2. I didn't *arrive home* until almost eight o'clock.   _____
3. He *entered* the elevator as soon as the door opened.   _____
4. How long will it take you to *prepare* for the party?   _____
5. The plane *arrives in* Washington about noon.   _____
6. She always *boards* the bus at this corner.   _____
7. She always *leaves* the bus at 79th Street.   _____
8. I *become very tired* if I have to walk too far.   _____
9. Helen *became excited* when she heard the good news.   _____
10. It took her several months to *recover from* the death of her friend.   _____
11. John *entered* the automobile first, and then I followed him.   _____
12. I usually *arrive at* my office at about nine o'clock.   _____
13. I seldom *reach home* before seven o'clock.   _____
14. Mr. Smith drank so much wine that I thought he was going to *become drunk*.   _____
15. They plan to *marry* in June.   _____
16. I always *become nervous* before an examination.   _____

58 Silent letters

For each of the words below, write the consonant that is written but not pronounced.

1.	knife	*k*	26.	write	_____
2.	answer	*w*	27.	fasten	_____
3.	handsome	_____	28.	castle	_____
4.	Christmas	_____	29.	hymn	_____
5.	island	_____	30.	scissors	_____
6.	doubt	_____	31.	lamb	_____
7.	knee	_____	32.	gnaw	_____
8.	wrestle	_____	33.	limb	_____
9.	honest	_____	34.	wrong	_____
10.	often	_____	35.	wrist	_____
11.	knew	_____	36.	listen	_____
12.	sign	_____	37.	sword	_____
13.	dumb	_____	38.	comb	_____
14.	match	_____	39.	knot	_____
15.	walk	_____	40.	kneel	_____
16.	could	_____	41.	czar	_____
17.	talk	_____	42.	half	_____
18.	knock	_____	43.	ghost	_____
19.	know	_____	44.	whistle	_____
20.	Wednesday	_____	45.	scent	_____
21.	pneumonia	_____	46.	calf	_____
22.	climb	_____	47.	ledge	_____
23.	should	_____	48.	hour	_____
24.	aisle	_____	49.	scene	_____
25.	whole	_____	50.	thumb	_____

mistakes of fact 2

The items in boldface are mistakes. Change them to make the facts correct, and write your answers in the blanks.

1. There are **eleven** months in a year.   *twelve*
2. The opposite of *thick* is **narrow.**   _____
3. To board a train is to **get off** it.   _____
4. Grass is generally **red** in color.   _____
5. The word *sleepy* is **a noun.**   _____
6. December is the **tenth** month of the year.   _____
7. The opposite of *loose* is **find.**   _____
8. The opposite of *safe* is **careless.**   _____
9. In the word *wrist* the letter **r** is silent
   (not pronounced).   _____
10. A triangle is a geometrical figure having **four** sides. _____
11. To *call on* someone is to **telephone** him or her.   _____
12. The Pacific Ocean lies **east** of the United States.   _____
13. The sun always sets in the **east.**   _____
14. Grapes grow on **trees.**   _____
15. We always buy and sell eggs by the **pound.**   _____
16. The term of office of the president of the United States
    is **six** years.   _____
17. There are **thirty-nine** inches in a yard.   _____
18. **Mr.** is a title for a married or unmarried woman.   _____
19. A common English proverb is "A stitch in time saves
    eight."   _____
20. Columbus discovered America in **1482.**   _____
21. The past participle of the verb *to be* is **was.**   _____
22. The past participle of the verb *to see* is **saw.**   _____

Write the correct prepositions or particles in the blanks.

1. He is not interested _____ English.   *in*

2. We arrived _____ Boston at exactly six o'clock.   _____

3. She lives far _____ the station.   _____

4. We went to the beach in spite _____ the bad weather.   _____

5. Sue sits _____ front of me in chemistry class.   _____

6. The police officer ran _____ the thief but could not
    catch him.   _____

7. Roger is mad _____ me because I won't go to the beach
    with him.   _____

8. Ana is always trying to borrow money _____ someone.   _____

9. I'll be back _____ an hour.   _____

10. It is dark in this room. Please turn _____ the light.   _____

11. The wind blew my hat _____.   _____

12. The dog tried to jump _____ the fence, but the fence
    was too high for him.   _____

13. The man died _____ pneumonia.   _____

14. They called off the game because _____ rain.   _____

15. Her English is improving little _____ little.   _____

16. The teacher crossed _____ several words in my
    composition.   _____

17. The vending machine is not working today.
    It must be out _____ order.   _____

18. Al did not do very well _____ his last exam.   _____

19. Maureen is very enthusiastic _____ her new job.   _____

20. He left his hat _____ the chair.   _____

21. He likes to walk _____ the rain.   _____

22. Rosemary plays the piano _____ ear.   _____

23. We plan to go to Chicago _____ plane.   _____

24. She is the girl I spoke to you _____.   _____

Select the correct answer and write it in the space provided.

1. We pronounce the contraction *he'd* to rhyme with (head, need, had, nod).   *need*

2. Tomatoes grow (on trees, on vines, in the ground, on bushes).   _____

3. We pronounce the word *please* to rhyme with (police, this, cease, breeze).   _____

4. To *get over* something means to (end, return to, need, recover from) it.   _____

5. What is the corresponding noun form of the verb to *succeed*?   _____

6. Which of the following animals is used mainly in the desert: giraffe, elephant, camel, cow?   _____

7. Which of the following is a popular dessert in the United States: roast beef, apple pie, chocolate milk, celery?   _____

8. We pronounce the word *said* to rhyme with (laid, sad, made, bed).   _____

9. Which of the following past tense forms do we pronounce as a word of only one syllable: counted, wanted, asked, needed, planted.   _____

10. Which letter in the word *ghost* is silent (not pronounced)?   _____

11. Which letter in the word *knit* is silent (not pronounced)?   _____

12. Which of these past tense forms do we pronounce as a word of two syllables: asked, changed, burned, pointed?   _____

13. In an airplane, which section is the cheapest: business class, coach, first class?   _____

14. The word *exhausted* has three syllables; on which of these three syllables do we accent the word?   _____

15. *Lately* means (very late, hardly ever, recently, seldom).   _____

16. Which one of these words is not spelled correctly: berth, shouted, garantee, reservation, interpreter?   _____

17. Which of these is a past participle: went, came, saw, did, gone?   _____

Select the correct form. Write your answers in the blanks.

1. They (was, were) both sitting in the park when I saw them.   *were*

2. When I met him, he already (has had, had had) his lunch.   _____

3. Ali (saved, has saved) $500 since January.   _____

4. Last night, while we (went, were going) to the movies, we met some old friends.   _____

5. Nina (went, has gone) to the dance with Sal last night.   _____

6. With (who, whom) did you go to the movies last night?   _____

7. Orchids, (who, which) are very beautiful, are difficult to grow.   _____

8. She asked (me to wait, that I wait) for her.   _____

9. He (said, told) that he would be back at six o'clock.   _____

10. She said her last name (is, was) Castro.   _____

11. He said that he (will, would) wait for us after the class.   _____

12. Ruth sat (between, among) Sachiko and Stephanie.   _____

13. Liz always (sits, is sitting) at this desk.   _____

14. Look! It (begins, is beginning) to snow.   _____

15. (Not, No) one student from our group attended the meeting.   _____

16. He asked me what (was my name, my name was).   _____

17. She spends (a lot of, many) time on her English.   _____

18. He has always been a good friend of (her, hers).   _____

19. Yesterday I met an old classmate of (me, my, mine).   _____

20. He (said, told) us that he would meet us at noon.   _____

21. Chris was sick yesterday and (can, could) not come to class.   _____

22. When I got there, they (were having, had) dinner.   _____

In the passive voice, the subject receives the action of the verb. Form the passive voice by using the appropriate form of to be *and the past participle of the main verb.*

Active Voice	Passive Voice
He repairs my shoes.	My shoes *are repaired* by him.
He repaired my shoes.	My shoes *were repaired* by him.
He will repair my shoes.	My shoes *will be repaired* by him.
He has repaired my shoes.	My shoes *have been repaired* by him.

Change the following sentences from the active to the passive voice. Write complete sentences. Put all adverbial expressions at the end of the sentence.

1. Mr. Dodd teaches this class.   *This class is taught by Mr. Dodd.*

2. She writes many newspaper articles. _____

3. The maid cleans the room every day. _____

4. Everyone hears their quarrels. _____

5. The letter carrier delivers the mail. _____

6. The secretary writes all the letters. _____

7. Everyone enjoys her speeches. _____

8. They sell the magazine everywhere. _____

9. She corrects our exercises at home. _____

10. Joe prepares dinner every night. _____

11. They deliver the mail at ten o'clock. _____

12. A messenger brings urgent information. _____

13. They sign the documents in the attorney's office. _____

14. She brought presents from Hong Kong. _____

15. The teacher corrects our compositions. _____

16. They print the books in Boston. _____

17. He cuts the grass once a week. _____

18. They send the letters by overnight mail. _____

19. The lawyer prepares the contracts. _____

20. The foundation provides the money. _____

64 Passive voice 2

***The passive voice in the past perfect tense is formed in the
following way:***

> Akira Kurosawa had directed the movie.
> The movie *had been directed* by Akira Kurosawa.

*Change the following sentences from the active to the passive
voice. Write complete sentences. Put all adverbial expressions at the
end of the sentence.*

1. Mr. Sato taught
   the class yesterday. *The class was taught by Mr. Sato yesterday.*

2. Someone took the money. _____

3. The letter carrier had delivered
   the mail. _____

4. He has signed the letters. _____

5. She has written many books. _____

6. Marianne paid the bills by check. _____

7. They will finish the work
   tomorrow. _____

8. He had finished the work in time. _____

9. They have planned the party. _____

10. Native Americans grew corn
    in Mexico. _____

11. He has designed several
    buildings. _____

12. He had signed the contract
    previously. _____

13. She broke the plate while
    she was washing it. _____

14. Julia saw the accident on her
    way home from work. _____

15. They had bought the tickets. _____

16. They have found the child at last. _____

17. Sonia planted the trees. _____

18. They prepared the dinner. _____

19. She will send it immediately. _____

20. He used the key to
    open the door. _____

65 Passive voice 3

Form the passive voice of can, have to, may, must, ought to, **and** should **with** be **and the past participle of the main verb.**

I *must* finish this work quickly.	This work *must be finished* (by me) quickly.
You *can* protect the plants with plastic bags.	The plants *can be protected* (by you) with plastic bags.
She *should* do her work on a word processor.	Her work *should be done* (by her) on a word processor.

Form the passive voice with infinitives by using be **and the past participle of the main verb.**

He has *to do* it today.	It has *to be done* (by him) today.
They are going *to take* it.	It is going *to be taken* by them.

Form the passive in the continuous tenses with being **and the past participle of the main verb.**

She *is watering* the flowers.	The flowers *are being watered* by her.

If it is not important to state the doer of the action, the by **phrase can be omitted.**

Change the following sentences from the active to the passive voice. Write complete sentences. Leave out the by *phrase if the subject is a pronoun. Put all adverbial expressions at the end of the sentence.*

1. We can finish this today.   *This can be finished today.*
2. The museum may keep it for two weeks. _____
3. You can pay the bill later. _____
4. We have to deliver it tomorrow. _____
5. They can't put those things there. _____
6. They must send it at once. _____
7. They should deliver it today. _____
8. You ought to write it now. _____
9. Kevin must study these exercises. _____
10. They may bring it later. _____
11. Linda can use this room. _____
12. She has to do it soon. _____
13. The police may hold him for several days. _____

Form negatives in the passive voice by placing not **after the auxiliary verb. We generally use the contracted forms.**

> The book *was not written (wasn't written)* by Ian Fleming.
>
> The film *will not be shown (won't be shown)* until next week.

Change the following sentences to the negative form. Write the complete verb in the blanks.

1. The book was published in France.   *was not published*

2. The books will be delivered on Wednesday.   _____

3. These letters must be signed by the manager.   _____

4. The thief was shot by a police officer.   _____

5. This class is taught by Ellen Marks.   _____

6. The package was wrapped very neatly.   _____

7. The house was struck by lightning.   _____

8. The mail has been delivered.   _____

9. The war was followed by a serious economic depression.   _____

10. The screams were heard by everyone.   _____

11. This room can be used for our lesson.   _____

12. The book was printed in Mexico.   _____

13. The letters were sent by regular mail.   _____

14. The merchandise will be delivered tomorrow.   _____

15. The bill can be sent after the first of the month.   _____

16. The money was taken by one of the visitors.   _____

17. We were disappointed by the music.   _____

18. The report will be prepared by Joe Trumbull.   _____

19. All the work has been finished.   _____

20. The house had been decorated by a New York firm.   _____

67 Passive voice: question form

Form questions in the passive voice by placing the auxiliary verb before the subject.

> *Will* that film *be shown* on TV this year?
>
> *Was* the best actor award *won* by Robert De Niro?

Change the following sentences to the question form. Write the subject and the complete verb in the blanks.

1. The man was shot by a police officer.   *Was the man shot ?*

2. The thief was captured by the police.   _____

3. The lecture will be attended by many important people.   _____

4. The dinner has been served by the host.   _____

5. We are invited to David's party.   _____

6. The work will be done by a Santa Fe firm.   _____

7. The city was destroyed by fire.   _____

8. These letters must be signed at once.   _____

9. America was discovered in 1492.   _____

10. The house has been struck by lightning.   _____

11. The tree was blown down by the hurricane.   _____

12. They were arrested by the police.   _____

13. His book will be published next month.   _____

14. This project must be finished today.   _____

15. The mail is delivered at exactly nine o'clock.   _____

16. The poems are written by Connie.   _____

17. The car was destroyed in the accident.   _____

18. Their engagement will be announced soon.   _____

19. They will be married in New York.   _____

20. The meeting was held in Paris.   _____

21. It was attended by all the foreign ministers.   _____

22. All these books can be borrowed from the library.   _____

68 Review: articles

Write the definite or indefinite article in the blanks.
If no article is necessary, leave blank.

1. They say that _____ climate of Mexico
   is very pleasant.   *the*

2. I bought my new suit at _____ Macy's.   _____

3. I have such _____ headache that I can hardly see.   _____

4. How do you like that kind of _____ weather?   _____

5. I enjoy walking along _____ Ocean Avenue.   _____

6. _____ Bank Street pier is popular on weekends.   _____

7. May I have a glass of _____ cold water?   _____

8. _____ water in this glass is not cold.   _____

9. This is one of _____ longest rivers in the world.   _____

10. Susan is _____ engineer.   _____

11. I will meet you in front of _____
    Grand Central Station.   _____

12. _____ United States sent three astronauts
    to the moon in 1969.   _____

13. Have you ever visited _____ England?   _____

14. _____ English fought bravely in World War II.   _____

15. _____ English language is not difficult to learn.   _____

16. It was so hot _____ day that we had to stop work.   _____

17. It was such _____ hot day that we had to stop work.   _____

18. We walked along Fifth Avenue as far as _____
    Central Park.   _____

19. In general, it takes several years to learn _____
    foreign language.   _____

20. He is _____ Frenchman.   _____

21. This is _____ Dominique's book.   _____

22. _____ Dominican Republic lies east of Cuba.   _____

23. We took a trip around _____ Mediterranean.   _____

24. _____ President Grey had a serious heart attack.   _____

25. _____ president will speak on TV tonight.   _____

Study and memorize the list of irregular verbs below. Note that they terminate in an n *sound in the past participle form.*

grow	grew	grown	speak	spoke	spoken
hide	hid	hidden	steal	stole	stolen
know	knew	known	take	took	taken
lie	lay	lain	tear	tore	torn
ride	rode	ridden	throw	threw	thrown
see	saw	seen	wear	wore	worn
shake	shook	shaken	write	wrote	written

Write the correct form of the verb in the sentences below.

1. Someone broke into our house last night and (steal) our new television set.   *stole*
2. Look! You have (tear) your coat. _____
3. The dog has always (lie) in that position. _____
4. I have (know) Franco for many years. _____
5. After Michael introduced us, we (shake) hands. _____
6. Michel (speak) to me about that matter yesterday. _____
7. The child has (grow) more than six inches in the last year. _____
8. Pedro got angry and (throw) the book on the table. _____
9. The child ran and (hide) behind a tree. _____
10. She has (wear) that hat every day for months. _____
11. Last night I stayed at home and (write) several letters. _____
12. Carlos (take) Monique to the dance last night. _____
13. I haven't (ride) in Sachiko's new car yet. _____
14. He was born in Mexico but (grow) up in California. _____
15. I haven't (see) Nina in several weeks. _____
16. Clara (tear) up the letter and then threw it away. _____
17. Grace and Jane have not (speak) to each other for several months. _____
18. Paul (know) Spain well because he had been there many times before. _____
19. I believe he has (know) about it for a long time. _____
20. Giselle (wear) a nice ski outfit yesterday. _____

opposites 2

Write the opposites of the following words.

1.	loser	*winner*	26.	sweet	_____
2.	strong	_____	27.	tall	_____
3.	everyone	_____	28.	useless	_____
4.	alive	_____	29.	increase	_____
5.	false	_____	30.	follow	_____
6.	polite	_____	31.	parent	_____
7.	careful	_____	32.	front	_____
8.	stop	_____	33.	raise	_____
9.	remember	_____	34.	tragedy	_____
10.	wrong	_____	35.	same	_____
11.	early	_____	36.	east	_____
12.	never	_____	37.	rise	_____
13.	slow	_____	38.	depart	_____
14.	effect	_____	39.	lost	_____
15.	smooth	_____	40.	domestic	_____
16.	loosen	_____	41.	presence	_____
17.	wholesale	_____	42.	temporary	_____
18.	brave	_____	43.	victory	_____
19.	sell	_____	44.	private	_____
20.	quiet	_____	45.	enemy	_____
21.	dry	_____	46.	lend	_____
22.	tight	_____	47.	subtract	_____
23.	forward	_____	48.	guilty	_____
24.	complicated	_____	49.	common	_____
25.	empty	_____	50.	winter	_____

adverbs, comparative form

The comparative form of one-syllable adjectives and adverbs adds er.

cold–colder	fast–faster

The comparative form of adjectives and adverbs of more than one syllable usually uses more. **However, two-syllable adjectives that end in** y **or** ow **add** er. **The** y **is changed to** i **before the** er **is added.**

expensive–more expensive	needy–needier
rapidly–more rapidly	shallow–shallower

Remember the irregular forms of the following adjectives and adverbs:

good–better	well–better
bad–worse	badly–worse

Write the comparative form of the following adjectives and adverbs + than.

1. Tokyo is (big) Chicago.   *bigger than*
2. Carmen is (intelligent) her sister. _____
3. He arrived (early) we expected. _____
4. This book is (interesting) that one. _____
5. The Amazon River is much (wide) the Orinoco River. _____
6. This exercise is (easy) the last one. _____
7. She sings (beautiful) her sister. _____
8. She drives even (fast) her father. _____
9. He returned (soon) we expected. _____
10. Some people speak English (clear) others. _____
11. He goes there (often) I. _____
12. Your pronunciation is (good) Clara's. _____
13. The weather today is (cold) it was yesterday. _____
14. She is (busy) she has ever been before. _____
15. Diego works (hard) the other students. _____
16. She prepares her lessons (careful) they. _____
17. They go to the movies (often) we. _____
18. I got up this morning (early) usual. _____
19. Oranges are (sweet) lemons. _____
20. Prices are (high) they have ever been. _____

*As. . .as **expresses equality. The phrase may be used with both adjectives and adverbs.***

> Lisa is *as* tall *as* Doug.
>
> Martin can run *as* fast *as* you can.
>
> I left the office *as* soon *as* I could.

Supply the phrase as. . .as, *and change adjectives to their corresponding adverb form where necessary.*

1. Tomiko is (tall) her brother.   *as tall as*
2. This book was (expensive) that one.   _____
3. Mario is not (old) I.   _____
4. She can speak English (good) the teacher.   _____
5. Amanda can't swim (fast) I.   _____
6. I will be there (soon) possible.   _____
7. I did (good) I could on the examination.   _____
8. The boy ran home (fast) his legs could carry him.   _____
9. Telephone me (soon) you get home.   _____
10. I don't think it is (cold) it was yesterday.   _____
11. He came to the office (quick) he could.   _____
12. She can do the work (easy) I.   _____
13. I am not (tired) I was yesterday.   _____
14. She doesn't work (hard) the other students.   _____
15. Your pronunciation is certainly (good) mine.   _____
16. We go to the movies (often) we can.   _____
17. Naturally, I cannot speak English (rapid) the teacher.   _____
18. I do my homework (careful) I can.   _____
19. She plays the piano (beautiful) anyone I have ever heard.   _____
20. He is almost (rich) the queen.   _____
21. She visits us (often) she can.   _____
22. I telephoned you (soon) I could.   _____

73 Review:

some-any/someone-anyone

Use some **in affirmative sentences. Use** any **in negative sentences.**

We took *some* money with us.	We didn't have *any* money with us.

Use someone, somebody, something, somewhere **in affirmative sentences. Use** anyone, anybody, anything, anywhere **in negative sentences.**

I saw *someone* standing in the shadows.	The witness said she hadn't seen *anything*.

Choose the correct form, and write it in the blanks.

1. He doesn't have (some, any) friends there.   *any*
2. The police found him (somewhere, anywhere) in Central Park.   _____
3. I didn't see (someone, anyone) in Ms. Stein's office.   _____
4. I didn't have (some, any) time to prepare my homework last night.   _____
5. Irene has (some, any) very pretty Persian carpets.   _____
6. Don't tell (someone, anyone) about this.   _____
7. Rita didn't say (something, anything) to me about it.   _____
8. I gave the old man (some, any) money.   _____
9. He met her (somewhere, anywhere) in Europe.   _____
10. I didn't have (some, any) money with me at the time.   _____
11. My aunt didn't send me (something, anything) for my birthday.   _____
12. I hear (someone, anyone) in the next room.   _____
13. Juan said that he hadn't seen (someone, anyone) in the room.   _____
14. There are (some, any) people waiting to see you.   _____
15. The police refuse to let (someone, anyone) see the prisoner.   _____
16. Mr. and Mrs. Garcia don't have (some, any) children.   _____
17. We didn't see (someone, anyone) we knew at the concert.   _____
18. I lost my purse (somewhere, anywhere) between here and 79th Street.   _____

Study and memorize the pronunciation of each word listed below. Write the number of syllables of each word in the first column. Write an ordinal number in the second column to tell which syllable of each word is stressed (accented).

	Number of Syllables	Stressed Syllable
1. tomorrow	*3*	*2nd*
2. newspaper		
3. cafeteria		
4. communicate		
5. continuous		
6. admiration		
7. discovery		
8. president		
9. dangerous		
10. medicine		
11. repeated		
12. appeared		
13. imagination		
14. government		
15. announced		
16. disappointed		
17. important		
18. suggestion		
19. returned		
20. discovered		
21. unable		
22. popularity		
23. carriage		

Write the correct verb form in each of the following sentences.

1. They (have) dinner when we arrived.   *were having*

2. I saw clearly that, a few miles back, we (take) the wrong road.   _____

3. Eric always (get up) at the same time every morning.   _____

4. I (see) Helen at the airport yesterday.   _____

5. But I (not see) her since then.   _____

6. Sally, who is in the hospital, (be) there for more than a month.   _____

7. We (live) in Palo Alto from 1965 to 1975.   _____

8. What _____ you (do) when I telephoned you?   _____

9. Listen! Someone (knock) at the door.   _____

10. When we lived in San Diego, we often (take) trips by car to Mexico.   _____

11. Please be more quiet. The baby (sleep).   _____

12. The sun always (rise) in the east.   _____

13. Up to now, I (not be) farther west than Chicago.   _____

14. Lee said that he already (see) that movie.   _____

15. I met a friend yesterday whom I (not see) in five years.   _____

16. We (live) in France when the war broke out.   _____

17. Columbus, when he died, did not realize that he (discover) a new continent.   _____

18. Look! The tree (begin) to bloom.   _____

19. Isn't that Antonia who (cross) the street?   _____

20. We (arrive) at school every morning at eight o'clock.   _____

21. I was frightened because people (run) and screaming all around me.   _____

22. Ruth Davila (teach) in that school ever since she graduated from college.   _____

23. Art says that he (come) back again tomorrow.   _____

24. Gabriela said that she (come) back again tomorrow.   _____

25. I (see) him when I return.   _____

mistakes of fact 3

The items in boldface are mistakes. Change them to make the facts correct, and write your answers in the blanks.

1. The last month of the year is **November**.   *December*
2. There are **fourteen** inches in a foot.   _____
3. The section which we call New England is situated in the **northwestern** part of the United States.   _____
4. The longest river in the United States is the **Hudson** River.   _____
5. We accent the word *invitation* on the **fourth** syllable.   _____
6. We accent the word *composition* on the **second** syllable.   _____
7. The word *quickly* is an **adjective**.   _____
8. In the United States, Independence Day is celebrated on **November 27**.   _____
9. The verb *see* is the kind of verb called **regular**.   _____
10. Canada lies **south** of the United States.   _____
11. The largest state in the United States is **California**.   _____
12. The smallest state in the United States is **Delaware**.   _____
13. To form the present perfect tense in English, we use the verb *have* as an auxiliary verb, and to this auxiliary we add the **present participle** of the main verb.   _____
14. The past tense of the verb *lie* is **laid**.   _____
15. The past tense of the verb *sit* is **set**.   _____
16. The past participle of the verb *go* is **went**.   _____
17. In the United States, Thanksgiving is celebrated in the **spring**.   _____
18. We pronounce the word *walked* as a word of **two syllables**.   _____
19. The superlative form of the adjective *bad* is **worse**.   _____
20. March is the **fourth** month of the year.   _____
21. In the United States, we celebrate Abraham Lincoln's birthday in **May**.   _____
22. In the United States, when we speak of the Father of His Country, we are referring to **Abraham Lincoln**.   _____

Write the correct prepositions or particles in the blanks.

1. Both Alice and Marianne were absent _____ school yesterday.   *from*

2. Lucia bought a ticket _____ Chicago at the station.   _____

3. I'll be over to see you _____ Wednesday night.   _____

4. We have decided to put _____ our trip until next month.   _____

5. What is the word _____ eggs in Spanish?   _____

6. He plans to take a trip _____ the world next year.   _____

7. A scarecrow is supposed to drive birds away _____ the garden.   _____

8. What time do you get home _____ school every day?   _____

9. Our team was playing _____ the team from the next town.   _____

10. He stuck the stamps _____ the envelope.   _____

11. This is an exception _____ the rule.   _____

12. He threw a stone and hit me _____ the eye.   _____

13. He took the child _____ the hand and helped her to cross the street.   _____

14. You can always depend _____ Rose.   _____

15. He asked the druggist to give him something _____ a headache.   _____

16. He doesn't understand a word _____ English.   _____

17. I met Catherine _____ my way to school.   _____

18. They laughed _____ the story I had told.   _____

19. The buses are always crowded _____ this time of day.   _____

20. The woman who waited _____ us was very polite.   _____

21. The package was too heavy _____ her to carry.   _____

22. He smiled _____ me in a very friendly way.   _____

23. We could see them _____ the distance.   _____

Select the correct answer and write it in the space provided.

1. If someone goes somewhere *for good*, he or she goes there (on a vacation, for health reasons, for a change, permanently).

   permanently

2. *On account of* has the same meaning as (instead of, in front of, in need of, because of).

   _____

3. *Once in a while* means (sometimes, for a long time, seldom, forever).

   _____

4. In which of these words is the letter *s* pronounced like *z*: miss, pass, was, this?

   _____

5. *Pretty good* means (very good, rather good, awfully good, not at all good).

   _____

6. The word *tough* is pronounced to rhyme with (cough, love, enough, ought).

   _____

7. The opposite of *rough* is (shiny, lean, smooth, easy).

   _____

8. Potatoes grow in the ground, but tomatoes grow on (trees, bushes, vines, fences).

   _____

9. What is the corresponding noun form of the verb *explain*?

   _____

10. What is the corresponding adjective form of the noun *curiosity*?

    _____

11. Which one of the following verbs is a regular verb: see, take, swim, come, count?

    _____

12. To shave, a person needs a (knife, fork, map, razor, string).

    _____

13. We pronounce the contraction *she'll* to rhyme with (shell, will, pale, heel).

    _____

14. Which of these words is a synonym for *student*: child, orphan, companion, pupil?

    _____

15. Which of these has the lowest army rank: corporal, sergeant, lieutenant, captain?

    _____

16. What is the plural form of *mouse*?

    _____

17. What is the plural form of *sheep*?

    _____

Select the correct form. Write your answers in the blanks.

1. There (was, were) several students absent from class
   this morning.   *were*

2. Angela (slept, was sleeping) when I telephoned her.   _____

3. We (are going, go) to school on the bus every morning.   _____

4. He (is, has been) in the hospital for several weeks.   _____

5. She is a very old friend of (me, my, mine).   _____

6. He wants (that we wait, us to wait) for him after
   the lesson.   _____

7. Isn't that Carlos who (waits, is waiting) in line?   _____

8. She said that she (can, could) speak French.   _____

9. The police refuse to let (someone, anyone) visit
   the prisoner.   _____

10. She works much harder (as, than) the other students.   _____

11. She is (a, an) honest woman.   _____

12. He is also (a, an) very honest person.   _____

13. He wanted to know where (I lived, did I live).   _____

14. When I got there, they (had, were having) dinner.   _____

15. He (said, told) that he would call me later.   _____

16. She didn't think that she (can, could) go with us.   _____

17. I thought that I (may, might) not be able to get
    there in time to see him.   _____

18. Adela sent (her, to her) some beautiful flowers.   _____

19. Hurry! The bus (comes, is coming) around the corner.   _____

20. They (have, are having) their music lesson now.   _____

21. They always (have, are having) their music lesson on
    Tuesday at this time.   _____

22. They (spent, have spent) two months in Mexico
    last winter.   _____

23. The teacher explained (us, to us) the correct meaning
    of the word.   _____

24. They (are, have been) very good friends for many years. _____

Study and memorize the forms of the following irregular verbs.

begin	began	begun	sing	sang	sung
drink	drank	drunk	sink	sank	sunk
ring	rang	rung	spring	sprang	sprung
shrink	shrank	shrunk	swim	swam	swum

The following verbs have the same form for the present tense, the past tense, and the past participle. Study and memorize them.

bet	cut	let	shut
burst	hit	put	split
cost	hurt	set	spread

Write the correct form of the verb in the sentences below.

1. The meeting had already (begin) when we arrived.   *begun*
2. We (sing) all the latest popular songs last night.   _____
3. The telephone (ring) just as I was leaving home.   _____
4. We will (set) the table for dinner later.   _____
5. Felipe (put) on his coat and left the room.   _____
6. It has (begin) to rain very hard.   _____
7. Has the school bell (ring) yet?   _____
8. Paolo (hurt) himself playing soccer yesterday.   _____
9. Mr. Wong has (drink) his medicine already.   _____
10. The teacher (let) us go home early yesterday.   _____
11. The ship had already (sink) when help arrived.   _____
12. Pina's dress (shrink) when she washed it.   _____
13. The cat (spring) upon the mouse and killed it instantly.   _____
14. Joan has (put) every cent she has into that business.   _____
15. We went to the beach yesterday and (swim) in the ocean for several hours.   _____
16. Have you ever (cut) yourself badly with a knife?   _____
17. The boy threw a stone at his companion and (hit) him in the eye.   _____
18. The news of the explosion last night (spread) quickly.   _____
19. It has (cost) her a great deal of money to educate her five children.   _____

*Supposed to, **used with the simple form of the main verb,** **expresses anticipation, expectation, or obligation. It can** **be used in the past and present tenses.***

> Julia *is supposed to* get there before the weekend. (present)
>
> We *were supposed to* mail you the package last week, but we just mailed it today. (past)

Write the correct form of supposed to *in the sentences below. Include the main verb in your answer.*

1. We (spend) two hours on our homework every night.   *are supposed to spend*

2. He (leave) for Chicago last night, but he was delayed.   _____

3. I (arrive) at school every day at nine o'clock.   _____

4. Maria (be) here now.   _____

5. We (go) to Florida next week.   _____

6. Everyone (bring) a friend to the meeting tomorrow.   _____

7. She (telephone) me yesterday, but apparently she forgot.   _____

8. We (write) a composition for tomorrow's class.   _____

9. The maid (clean) this room every morning.   _____

10. The train (arrive) two hours ago.   _____

11. Patrick (be) in Paris next month.   _____

12. The plane (leave) last night at midnight, but bad weather delayed it.   _____

13. They (deliver) the merchandise yesterday.   _____

14. She (call) me long distance from New York last night.   _____

15. This building (be) open to the public every day.   _____

16. June (leave) for Chicago next Wednesday.   _____

17. She (stay) there for about two weeks and then go on to California.   _____

18. They (publish) the book last October.   _____

82 Used to

Used to *describes an action that was a habit in the past or which occurred often in the past but that does not happen at the present time. It can also describe a state in the past.*

> I *used to* smoke a pack a day. (Now I only smoke a cigarette after each meal).
>
> We *used to* live in Paris. (We moved and now we live in California).

In the blanks at the right, write the phrase used to *followed by the verb in parentheses.*

1. I (play) tennis well when I was a girl.   *used to play*
2. They (live) across the street from us.   _____
3. She and I (be) good friends.   _____
4. We (walk) to school together every day.   _____
5. He (work) for my father.   _____
6. She (be) one of the smartest girls in town.   _____
7. They (visit) us every summer.   _____
8. He (go) to Europe quite often.   _____
9. She (study) in our group.   _____
10. He (be) a teacher before he went into business.   _____

Substitute a verb phrase with used to *for the italicized verbs. Write answers in the blanks at the right.*

11. He *spent* too much time studying.   *used to spend*
12. She *visited* us.   _____
13. He *played* the violin well.   _____
14. She *sent* her mother flowers.   _____
15. He *wrote* articles for the newspapers.   _____
16. I *caught* cold when I went out in the rain.   _____
17. She *helped* me with my lessons.   _____
18. We *danced* until dawn.   _____
19. She *took* Grace to school.   _____
20. I *walked* two miles to school.   _____

83 Short answers

Short answers are the most common form of answering direct questions. (They are also considered more polite than a simple yes or no answer.) A short answer consists of the subject of the sentence and an auxiliary verb or part of to be. *If there is no auxiliary verb, the verb* to do *is used.*

Can you play tennis?	Yes, I can.	No, I can't.
Do you know my friend?	Yes, I do.	No, I don't.
Is she at home?	Yes, she is.	No, she isn't.
Did Henry call you?	Yes, he did.	No, he didn't.

Note that pronouns are used to replace the noun when the short answer is used.

Write affirmative and negative short answers for the questions below. Answer you *questions with* I, *and answer* you and X *questions with* we.

1. Did you do your homework last night?   *Yes, I did.*   *No, I didn't.*

2. Is the sun shining?   _____   _____

3. Did it rain hard last night?   _____   _____

4. Is Alice a good teacher?   _____   _____

5. Have you and Will ever been to Mexico?   _____   _____

6. Can Mercedes play tennis well?   _____   _____

7. Does it often rain during April?   _____   _____

8. Is Roger supposed to be here now?   _____   _____

9. Have you and Nora had your dinner yet?   _____   _____

10. Will you be in class tomorrow?   _____   _____

11. Are you going to the movies tonight?   _____   _____

12. Does Christine speak English well?   _____   _____

13. Were you late for your lesson?   _____   _____

14. Was Adela always such a good student?   _____   _____

15. Can Ricardo speak French well?   _____   _____

84 Tag questions 1

Tag questions invite confirmation of a statement. They contain an auxiliary verb and a pronoun. Affirmative tag questions are used after negative statements; negative tag questions are used after affirmative statements.

> You live in the city, don't you?
> They had a long trip, didn't they?
> You will be at the dinner, won't you?
> Maria can speak Spanish, can't she?

In there is/are **statements, treat** there **like a subject.**

Add the correct tag questions to the following sentences.

1. Mario left for Chicago last night, _____?   *didn't he*
2. She is a very good lawyer, _____?   _____
3. There are many students absent today, _____?   _____
4. You wrote those letters, _____?   _____
5. The traffic will be very heavy, _____?   _____
6. Ana can help us, _____?   _____
7. It was a good movie, _____?   _____
8. He has been your teacher for a long time, _____?   _____
9. He is a very nice fellow, _____?   _____
10. That dog is yours, _____?   _____
11. The bus stops on this corner, _____?   _____
12. You gave me my change, _____?   _____
13. I paid you, _____?   _____
14. Angela is an excellent teacher, _____?   _____
15. She has studied English for many years, _____?   _____
16. Your father is an engineer, _____?   _____
17. You will be in class tomorrow, _____?   _____
18. It was raining at the time, _____?   _____
19. He is supposed to leave tomorrow, _____?   _____
20. You have had your lunch, _____?   _____

Remember that affirmative tag questions are used after negative statements.

> You don't live in the city, do you?
> They didn't have a long trip, did they?
> You won't be at the dinner, will you?
> Maria can't speak Spanish, can she?

Add the correct tag questions to the following sentences.

1. The plane didn't arrive on time, _____?   *did it*
2. The bus doesn't stop on this corner, _____?   _____
3. He is not a very dependable person, _____?   _____
4. Norma can't go with us, _____?   _____
5. You won't be back before noon, _____?   _____
6. It wasn't raining at the time, _____?   _____
7. You haven't had your dinner yet, _____?   _____
8. His wife didn't come with him, _____?   _____
9. You can't speak French, _____?   _____
10. You don't know how to swim, _____?   _____
11. He doesn't like to go to the beach, _____?   _____
12. She won't be able to go with us, _____?   _____
13. You haven't ever been to Europe, _____?   _____
14. It hasn't begun to rain, _____?   _____
15. Your roof doesn't leak, _____?   _____
16. You weren't driving fast at the time, _____?   _____
17. Marcella wasn't hurt badly in the accident, _____?   _____
18. The mail hasn't been delivered yet, _____?   _____
19. It hasn't rained hard in a long time, _____?   _____
20. You won't mention this to anyone, _____?   _____

86 Tag questions 3

Add the correct tag questions to the following sentences.

1. She always goes to New York by plane, _____? *doesn't she*
2. Today isn't Wednesday, _____? _____
3. His father is a rather well-known lawyer, _____? _____
4. You saw that movie, _____? _____
5. He won't be back until Wednesday, _____? _____
6. It rains a lot during the month of April, _____? _____
7. They have a very pretty home, _____? _____
8. She is a surgeon, _____? _____
9. You'll be in class tomorrow, _____? _____
10. Your watch has stopped, _____? _____
11. I paid you the money I owed you, _____? _____
12. Bill hasn't been here today, _____? _____
13. He didn't telephone you, _____? _____
14. She dances very well, _____? _____
15. They have already left for Chicago, _____? _____
16. You spoke to Sue about that matter, _____? _____
17. She can meet us after the lesson, _____? _____
18. He promised to be here at noon, _____? _____
19. You haven't had your lunch yet, _____? _____
20. The car skidded, _____? _____
21. But it was the driver's fault, _____? _____
22. You see him at church on Sundays, _____? _____
23. It has been a beautiful day, _____? _____
24. He never mentioned it again, _____? _____
25. She doesn't like to go to the beach, _____? _____

A gerund is a form of verb which is used as a noun and ends in ing. **Certain verbs, like** enjoy, mind, stop, consider, appreciate, **and** finish, **can be followed by gerunds but not by infinitives.**

Gerund Form	*Infinitive Form*
I liked *walking.*	I like *to walk.*
I tried *calling* you.	I tried *to call* you.
She enjoys *swimming.*	They have finished *painting.*

Supply the gerund form of the verb in the following sentences.

1. We appreciate (hear) from you.   *hearing*
2. The man denied (take) the money.   _____
3. We cannot risk (invest) so much money.   _____
4. The driver could not avoid (hit) the curb.   _____
5. We are considering (move) to Miami.   _____
6. They have already finished (eat).   _____
7. We both enjoy (dance) very much.   _____
8. Do you mind (come) back later?   _____
9. He admitted (hide) the money.   _____
10. She says she doesn't mind (wait) for us.   _____
11. Steve and Tom have stopped (speak) to each other.   _____
12. We enjoy (listen) to music.   _____
13. He is going to stop (study) English.   _____
14. We will enjoy (use) your cottage at the beach while
    you are away.   _____
15. They have finally finished (paint) our apartment.   _____
16. Would you mind (open) the window?   _____
17. She denied (change) the address on the package.   _____
18. We are considering (buy) a new car.   _____
19. We would appreciate (receive) your answer
    immediately.   _____
20. He finally admitted (make) the mistake.   _____
21. I don't mind (ride) the subway.   _____

88 Gerunds 2

The following verbs may be followed by both gerunds and infinitives:

start	begin	continue	like	neglect
hate	try	love	prefer	intend

Complete the following sentences, once with the gerund and then with the infinitive.

1. She loves (work) for herself.   *working*   *to work*

2. He intends (leave) tomorrow.   _____   _____

3. She will try (study) in the library.   _____   _____

4. They will start (work) there next week.   _____   _____

5. She hates (do) secretarial work.   _____   _____

6. She will continue (work) in that same office until June.   _____   _____

7. He prefers (dance) with his wife.   _____   _____

8. I neglected (mention) it to Bill.   _____   _____

9. He likes (teach) English to foreign students.   _____   _____

10. They will begin (build) their new home soon.   _____   _____

11. He prefers (watch) television.   _____   _____

12. She intends (stay) right where she is.   _____   _____

13. He loves (criticize) others.   _____   _____

14. We tried (find) an apartment near the park.   _____   _____

15. They have finally started (speak) to each other.   _____   _____

16. Rose loves (do) that kind of work.   _____   _____

17. They continue (send) us a bill for the work.   _____   _____

Gerunds may be used after most prepositions in the same way as nouns.

> I am fond of *hiking*.
> You use this lever for *turning* on the heat.

Gerunds are used after the expressions to be worth, no use, **and** do you mind.

> Your ideas *are* certainly *worth considering*.
> It's *no use worrying* about it. It doesn't affect us.
> *Do you mind closing* the window? I'm cold.

Supply the correct preposition and the gerund form of the verb in the following sentences.

1. We are thinking (move) to Miami.   *of moving*
2. She got tired (wait) for her.   _____
3. We are both very fond (dance).   _____
4. He insisted (go) with us.   _____
5. There is no chance (see) him today.   _____
6. We are excited (go) to Europe.   _____
7. It is a question (find) a good teacher.   _____
8. We all need more lessons (speak).   _____
9. We are looking forward (see) you again.   _____
10. She has had no instruction (teach).   _____
11. He takes great pleasure (help) others.   _____
12. She insisted (help) me.   _____
13. He has no intention (leave) the class.   _____
14. We are all interested (learn) English.   _____
15. Are you fond (swim)?   _____
16. We were finally successful (locate) him.   _____
17. We get tired (study) the same thing.   _____
18. We are thinking (buy) a new car.   _____
19. Is there any chance (see) Professor Frank today?   _____
20. We had no difficulty (find) where they lived.   _____
21. She has a talent (manage) children.   _____

Write the correct form of the verb in the sentences below.

1. It has (begin) to rain very hard.   *begun*
2. That dog has (bit) several people.   _____
3. The teacher (let) us go home early yesterday.   _____
4. All the birds have (fly) south for the winter.   _____
5. At our club meeting last night,
    we (choose) Rolando as our new president.   _____
6. Tom has (wear) that same hat for several years.   _____
7. While skating in the park yesterday,
    Henry (fall) and hurt himself.   _____
8. I have (give) them all the help I can.   _____
9. I caught my coat on a nail and (tear) it.   _____
10. I was born in Pennsylvania but (grow)
    up in New York.   _____
11. The boy ran and (hide) behind a tree.   _____
12. I have (know) Suzanne for many years.   _____
13. We have (drive) to Florida several times.   _____
14. We have already (sing) every old song we know.   _____
15. I stayed home last night and (write) some letters.   _____
16. During that storm last week, the wind (blow) down
    several trees in our block.   _____
17. We have (eat) in that restaurant several times.   _____
18. The police have not yet (find) out who
    stole the money.   _____
19. Our guide (lead) us through one government building
    after another yesterday.   _____
20. The dog has (lie) in that same spot all morning.   _____
21. I hope that you have not (throw) away those magazines
    I left here.   _____
22. The news of the accident yesterday (spread) quickly.   _____
23. The lake (freeze) over last week.   _____
24. They have not (speak) to each other in weeks.   _____

91 Idiomatic expressions

Select the correct answer and write it in the space provided.

1. To *look for* something is to (appreciate it, search for it, overlook it, look it up).   *search for it*

2. If someone goes somewhere for *good,* he or she goes there (for health reasons, to look for work, frequently, permanently).   _____

3. To *get on* a train is to (leave, board, inspect, walk through) it.   _____

4. To *call up* someone is to (wave to, criticize, respect, telephone) him or her.   _____

5. To *call on* someone is to (abuse, look down upon, visit, telephone) him or her.   _____

6. To *call for* someone is to (look up to, come for, name, send for) him or her.   _____

7. *I'd sooner study* means that I (dislike, hope, intend, prefer) to study.   _____

8. To *talk over* something is to (overlook, forget, repeat, discuss) it.   _____

9. To *look over* something is to (forget it, put it aside, examine it, postpone it).   _____

10. To be *about to do* something is to be (worried about doing, at the point of doing, opposed to doing) it.   _____

11. To *throw something away* is to (break, preserve, discard, need) it.   _____

12. *As yet* means (not at all, up to the present, suddenly, almost).   _____

13. To be *used to* something means to be (tired of, happy about, accustomed to, worried about) it.   _____

14. To *make believe* is to (pretend, discuss, withdraw, argue). _____

15. To be *mixed up* is to be (annoyed, amused, confused, disappointed).   _____

16. To learn something *by heart* is to learn it (quickly, slowly, carelessly, by memory).   _____

17. If someone says to you, "Look out!", this means (look out the window, be careful, sit down and rest).   _____

Many words are used as both nouns and verbs, with no change in their form.

Verb	Noun
They *work* here every day.	Their *work* is excellent.
We *need* peace in the world.	There is a *need* for world peace.

A few of the many English words besides those in this exercise that may be used as nouns and verbs without a change in form are the following: study, cry, help, drink, taste, wish, finish, tie, talk, kiss, smile, shout, play, surprise, start, walk, crowd, rest, fall, present, move, ride, watch, block, mistake, scream, curse, fire, fool, mark, result, call, offer, part, escape, play, time, fish, guide, mind, **and** point.

Write noun *if the italicized word of the sentence is used as a noun; write* verb *if the italicized word is used as a verb.*

1. We *look* very elegant in our new clothes.   *verb*

   We saw the *look* of surprise on his face.   _____

2. It is a *question* of finding the right person for the job.   _____

   The police are going to *question* everyone about the robbery.   _____

3. There is no *need* to discuss the matter further.   _____

   We *need* some new tires for our car.   _____

4. All children *love* candy.   _____

   His *love* for her will never die.   _____

5. The *sound* of the shot was heard by everyone.   _____

   Both men *sound* angry to me.   _____

6. Martha's *face* looked pale and drawn.   _____

   All the buildings in our block *face* the park.   _____

7. She *plans* to go to Europe in June.   _____

   Their *plans* to go to Europe in June fell through.   _____

8. Did you *notice* the new dress Joyce was wearing?   _____

   Each teacher received a *notice* of the change in examination dates.   _____

9. Why did you *promise* to help him?   _____

   Ned's *promise* to help you means nothing at all.   _____

Many words have different, though similar or related, forms as nouns and verbs. Study and memorize the differences as you write the corresponding noun forms of the verbs listed.

1. to decide   *decision*
2. to excite   *excitement*
3. to weigh   _____
4. to oblige   _____
5. to recognize   _____
6. to insist   _____
7. to repeat   _____
8. to locate   _____
9. to arrive   _____
10. to analyze   _____
11. to tempt   _____
12. to argue   _____
13. to adjust   _____
14. to react   _____
15. to expect   _____
16. to prove   _____
17. to describe   _____
18. to arrange   _____
19. to treat   _____
20. to consider   _____
21. to explain   _____
22. to annoy   _____

23. to appear   _____
24. to believe   _____
25. to breathe   _____
26. to confuse   _____
27. to inspect   _____
28. to admire   _____
29. to relieve   _____
30. to choose   _____
31. to embarrass   _____
32. to destroy   _____
33. to complete   _____
34. to satisfy   _____
35. to enjoy   _____
36. to hesitate   _____
37. to paralyze   _____
38. to identity   _____
39. to protect   _____
40. to obey   _____
41. to discover   _____
42. to complain   _____
43. to criticize   _____
44. to refuse   _____

and verb forms 2

Write the corresponding verb forms of the nouns listed.

1.	imagination	*to imagine*	25.	amusement	_____
2.	existence	*to exist*	26.	excitement	_____
3.	growth	_____	27.	robbery	_____
4.	interference	_____	28.	success	_____
5.	burial	_____	29.	punishment	_____
6.	explosion	_____	30.	decision	_____
7.	interruption	_____	31.	observation	_____
8.	disturbance	_____	32.	reservation	_____
9.	apology	_____	33.	adoption	_____
10.	admission	_____	34.	deception	_____
11.	repetition	_____	35.	remainder	_____
12.	proof	_____	36.	loss	_____
13.	collection	_____	37.	failure	_____
14.	relief	_____	38.	warning	_____
15.	impression	_____	39.	entrance	_____
16.	marriage	_____	40.	beginning	_____
17.	denial	_____	41.	withdrawal	_____
18.	intention	_____	42.	paralysis	_____
19.	choice	_____	43.	belief	_____
20.	approval	_____	44.	conclusion	_____
21.	advice	_____	45.	refusal	_____
22.	death	_____	46.	destruction	_____
23.	suspicion	_____	47.	criticism	_____
24.	agreement	_____	48.	complaint	_____

Write the correct prepositions in the blanks.

1. She is not interested _____ learning English.
   in

2. He is worried _____ his wife's health.
   _____

3. It is a question _____ getting permission from the authorities.
   _____

4. She insisted _____ helping me with the work.
   _____

5. For tomorrow's lesson, we will study from page ten _____ page fifteen.
   _____

6. He poured the wine _____ the glass.
   _____

7. The button fell _____ the shirt.
   _____

8. She said that, _____ the circumstances, she could do nothing for us.
   _____

9. He didn't mention anything to me _____ it.
   _____

10. We have been waiting for him _____ twenty minutes.
    _____

11. Paris is famous _____ its many art galleries.
    _____

12. I didn't interfere _____ his plans.
    _____

13. Don't lean _____ that fence; it's just been painted.
    _____

14. I mistook Jane _____ her sister.
    _____

15. I want to ask a favor _____ you.
    _____

16. He was absent _____ class yesterday.
    _____

17. Don't drink _____ that glass.
    _____

18. Her English is improving little _____ little.
    _____

19. Who will take care _____ your dog while you are away?
    _____

20. She should go _____ a diet.
    _____

21. His face is very familiar _____ me.
    _____

22. We'll have to postpone our trip _____ next month.
    _____

23. The game was called off because _____ rain.
    _____

24. Whom are they waiting _____?
    _____

25. Take the dog out _____ a walk.
    _____

Select the correct answer and write it in the space provided.

1. To *talk over* something is to (repeat, discuss, enjoy, forget) it.   *discuss*

2. The opposite of *temporary* is (soon, early, complicated, permanent).   _____

3. The word *sewed* is pronounced to rhyme with (rude, stewed, flowed, could).   _____

4. The word *scene* is pronounced to rhyme with (cent, tin, men, mean).   _____

5. Which of these words may be used as both a noun and a verb without any change in form: explode, agree, grow, sound, enter?   _____

6. Which of these is an irregular verb: talk, want, count, sing, paint?   _____

7. We pronounce the contraction *there's* to rhyme with (hers, fears, hairs, liars).   _____

8. My *niece* is my (second cousin, enemy, rival, brother's daughter).   _____

9. What is the corresponding noun form of the verb *choose?*   _____

10. What is the corresponding noun form of the verb *advise?*   _____

11. Which letter in the word *often* is not pronounced?   _____

12. Which letter in the word *autumn* is silent?   _____

13. Which of these do we use to sweep the floor: mop, dust rag, broom, soap?   _____

14. Which of these do you need in order to row a boat: sails, anchor, oars, portholes?   _____

15. To ride on a bus or streetcar, you must pay a (fee, lawyer, fare, debt).   _____

16. To get *used to* something is to get (sick of, annoyed at, accustomed to, tired of) it.   _____

17. A common synonym for *trousers* is (vest, pants, cuffs, sleeves).   _____

18. To whom do you take your watch when you want it repaired: tailor, jeweler, druggist, mechanic?   _____

Select the correct form. Write your answers in the blanks.

1. He insisted (to go, on going) with us.   *on going*

2. They are thinking (to move, of moving)
    to Oakland.   _____

3. We (have lived, lived) in this same apartment
    since June.   _____

4. She is not interested (to learn, in learning) English.   _____

5. Do you mind (to wait, waiting) a few minutes?   _____

6. We would appreciate (to hear, hearing) from you as soon
    as possible.   _____

7. They have finally finished (to paint, painting)
    our apartment.   _____

8. Listen! The train (comes, is coming).   _____

9. The baby (cries, is crying) frequently during the day.   _____

10. When I got up this morning,
    it (rained, was raining) hard.   _____

11. I am used to (study, studying) with Ms. Levine,
    and I don't want to change to another teacher.   _____

12. The train (supposed, is supposed) to arrive
    at midnight.   _____

13. He asked (that I go, me to go) with him.   _____

14. She is an old friend of (us, our, ours).   _____

15. The ship had already (sank, sunk) when help arrived.   _____

16. He asked me what time it (is, was).   _____

17. She said that she (can, could) not speak English well.   _____

18. He wants to know what time
    (will you, you will) return.   _____

19. I couldn't find my book (somewhere, anywhere).   _____

20. She (works, has worked) in that office for many years.   _____

21. He (studied, has studied) English for two years when he
    was in high school.   _____

22. When we arrived, they (watched, were watching)
    television.   _____

Questions in indirect speech are expressed as statements.

Direct:	Tamara asked, "Where *does* Sean *live?*"
Indirect:	Tamara asked where Sean *lived.*

When the direct question does not contain a question word, the indirect question requires the introduction of *if* **or** whether.

Direct:	Tamara asked, "Does Sean live here?"
Indirect:	Tamara asked *if* Sean lived here.
	Tamara asked *whether* Sean lived here.

Choose the correct form to complete the sentences below.

1. She asked me what time (was it, it was).   *it was*
2. Can you tell me what time (is it, it is).   _____
3. He wanted to know how old (I was, was I).   _____
4. She asked me when (would I, I would) return.   _____
5. Ask him what time (is it, it is).   *it is*
6. Tell her how old (are you, you are).   _____
7. Ask him why (was he, he was) late.   _____
8. I don't know where (does she live, she lives).   _____
9. He didn't tell me where (did she live, she lived).   _____
10. The teacher asked me where (was I, I was) going.   _____
11. I don't know how far (is it, it is) from here to Seville.   _____
12. She asked me how much (did I pay, I paid) for my car.   _____
13. Ask Marc where (is he, he is) going.   _____
14. Sheila asked me how (did I like, I liked) my new class.   _____
15. I don't know where (did Adam put, Adam put) all those old magazines.   _____
16. No one seems to know where (did she go, she went).   _____
17. Can you tell me how much (does this cost, this costs)?   _____
18. I forget where (did I put, I put) it.   _____
19. He asked us in which room (we had, did we have) our English lesson.   _____
20. I wonder what time (is it, it is).   _____

99 Should, ought to

Should **and** ought **to mean the same thing. They both express obligation. The contracted form** shouldn't **is normally used.**

> You *should spend* more time with your family.
>
> You *ought to spend* more time with your family.
>
> She *shouldn't (should not) smoke* so much.
>
> She *ought not to smoke* so much.

Should **and** ought **are less strong in meaning than** must. **Must has almost the force of a command.** Should **and** ought **suggest that one has the obligation to do a certain thing.**

Substitute ought to *for should in the sentences below. Write the complete verb.*

1. She *should attend* class more regularly.   *ought to attend*
2. I *should go* to bed earlier every night.   _____
3. He *should choose* his friends more carefully.   _____
4. She *should not talk* back to her parents.   _____
5. You *should not write* your compositions in pencil.   _____
6. She *should be* more careful of her health.   _____
7. They *should try* to arrive at school on time.   _____
8. We *should get* more physical exercise.   _____
9. She *should have* more respect for her parents.   _____
10. She *should not speak* to him in that way.   _____
11. Children *should obey* their parents.   _____
12. Rod *should not read* so much.   _____
13. I *should write* to my friends more often.   _____
14. He *should try* to put on some weight.   _____
15. They *should take* their studies more seriously.   _____
16. We *should go* home by bus instead of taxi.   _____
17. This letter *should be sent* at once.   _____
18. They *should arrive* at five o'clock.   _____
19. These letters *should be written* by Regina.   _____
20. He *should not spend* so much money.   _____

Form the past of sentences with should **and** ought to **by using** have **and the past participle of the main verb.**

> We *should be* more careful.
> We *should have been* more careful.
> He *ought to finish* his work quickly.
> He *ought to have finished* his work quickly.

Note that the past form of should **and** ought to **has a negative feeling, since it suggests that something that should have been done was not done.**

Change these sentences to the past form. Write the correct form of the verb in the blanks at the right.

1. Al *should study* more before his examinations.   *should have studied.*

2. You *should go* with me to visit them. _____

3. They *should arrive* at five o'clock. _____

4. You *should go* by plane. _____

5. She *should telephone* you more often. _____

6. This letter *should be sent* at once. _____

7. This package *should be delivered* immediately. _____

8. She *should be* more careful in handling such things. _____

9. You *should tell* me about it. _____

10. He *should go* to see a doctor at once. _____

11. This letter *should be written* on letterhead stationery. _____

12. He *should write* to us more often. _____

13. You *should telephone* the police. _____

14. She *should write* to her parents more often. _____

15. He *should spend* more time on his homework. _____

16. They *should not waste* so much time. _____

17. She *should be* more careful of her health. _____

18. They *should not tell* anyone about it. _____

19. She *should ask* permission first. _____

20. He *should not talk* so freely with everyone. _____

Change the following sentences with ought to *to the past tense. Remember that the simple form of the verb is changed to the perfect form.*

1. She *ought to study* much harder.   *ought to have studied*
2. You *ought to go* with me to visit them. _____
3. He *ought to travel* by plane. _____
4. We *ought to save* more money. _____
5. She *ought to be* more careful of her health. _____
6. He *ought to sign* these letters at once. _____
7. This letter *ought to be sent* by overnight mail. _____
8. She *ought not to talk* so much. _____
9. This package *ought to be delivered* right away. _____
10. These letters *ought to be faxed.* _____
11. He *ought to see* a doctor at once. _____
12. They *ought not to mention* it to anyone. _____
13. We *ought not to waste* so much valuable time. _____
14. You *ought to explain* it to her more carefully. _____
15. We *ought to telephone* him at once. _____
16. She *ought not to work* so hard. _____
17. This material *ought to be prepared* right away. _____
18. We *ought to telephone* the police. _____
19. She *ought to get* more rest. _____
20. You *ought to go* to bed earlier every night. _____
21. She *ought to write* to her parents more often. _____
22. These chairs *ought to be put* in the other room. _____

102 Conditional sentences,

future possible 1

A conditional sentence has two clauses: the dependent clause introduced by if **and the main clause.**

> If you study, you will pass your exam.
>
> If you lend me five dollars, I will pay you back tomorrow.

In future possible conditional sentences, the dependent clause is in the present tense, and the main clause is in the future tense. The modals can **and** may **may also be used in the main clause.**

Write the correct form of the verb in the dependent clause of the conditional sentences below.

1. If Beatrice (study) hard, she will surely graduate.   *studies*
2. If he (work) hard, he will pass his exam.   _____
3. If she (hurry), she will be able to go with us.   _____
4. If it (rain), we will not go to the beach.   _____
5. If Randy (come), he can help us.   _____
6. If you (attend) class regularly, you will learn English quickly.   _____
7. If the weather (be) nice tomorrow, we will go to the beach.   _____
8. If he (telephone) me, I will let you know.   _____
9. If I (see) her, I will give her your message.   _____
10. If it (not rain), we will go on a picnic tomorrow.   _____
11. If I (have) time, I will call you tomorrow.   _____
12. If they (leave) early, they can get there on time.   _____
13. If she (get) back before four, I will call you.   _____
14. If Colette (call), I will tell her about our plans.   _____
15. If he (not come), I don't know what we will do.   _____
16. If we (decide) to go swimming, we will give you a ring.   _____
17. If the weather (get) any colder, we will have to buy overcoats.   _____
18. If the dog (bite) him, he will have to go to the hospital.   _____
19. If you (have) time tomorrow, we can go to the ball game.   _____

future possible 2

Write the correct form of the verb in parentheses in order to complete the future possible conditional sentences.

1. If Sue studies hard, she (pass) her examination. *will pass*
2. If I have time tomorrow, I (visit) you. _____
3. If he doesn't hurry, we (miss) our train. _____
4. If the weather is good next week, we probably (go) hunting. _____
5. If it doesn't rain tomorrow, we (go) to the beach. _____
6. If you attend class regularly, you (learn) English quickly. _____
7. If they leave early enough, they (be) able to get tickets. _____
8. If Ann calls, I (tell) her about our change in plans. _____
9. If we decide to go to the beach, I (let) you know. _____
10. If it snows tonight, we (have) to stay at home all day tomorrow. _____
11. If the weather continues to be so cold, I (have) to buy some warmer clothing. _____
12. If I get a good grade on my examination, my parents (be) pleased. _____
13. If I have time, I (give) you a ring tomorrow. _____
14. If I have a car next summer, I (drive) to the beach every day. _____
15. If we have enough money, we (take) a trip abroad next summer. _____
16. If he works hard, he (earn) a lot of money in that job. _____
17. If they get married now, they (have) to live with his parents. _____
18. If Stella comes before I leave, I (explain) everything to her. _____
19. If you go to bed earlier, you (be) less tired. _____
20. If you practice every day, you (play) the piano well. _____

104 Conditional sentences,

present unreal 1

In present unreal conditional sentences, the dependent clause is in the past tense, and the main clause takes would, should, could, *or* might. *In the negative form, the contracted forms* (didn't, wouldn't, shouldn't, etc.) *are generally used. This kind of conditional sentence is used to talk about a situation which is purely hypothetical.*

> If Joseph *studied* hard, he *would pass* his exam.
>
> If it *snowed* in the middle of the summer, all the flowers *would die.*
>
> If you *listened* more, you *would learn* what the problems are.

Write the correct form of the verb in order to complete the present unreal conditional sentences below. Use contracted forms for negative sentences.

1. If Stan (spend) more time on his lessons, he would get better marks.

    spent

2. If I (have) more time, I would go to the beach every day.

    _____

3. If I (own) an automobile, I would take a trip to California.

    _____

4. If she (work) harder, she would get a better position.

    _____

5. If I (know) his telephone number, I would call him up.

    _____

6. If I (speak) French well, I would take a trip to France.

    _____

7. If she (go) to bed earlier, she would be less tired.

    _____

8. If he (pay) more attention in class, he would pass the course.

    _____

9. If I (know) how to drive, I would buy a car.

    _____

10. If we (study) together, we could prepare our homework more easily.

    _____

11. If she (like) languages, it would be easier for her to learn. _____

12. If they (have) more conversation practice, they would speak better.

    _____

13. If we (have) more time, we would make more progress. _____

14. If I (not have) to work tomorrow, I would go to the beach with you.

    _____

15. If he (not waste) so much time in class, he would make more progress.

    _____

16. If I (have) more money, I would spend it on travel. _____

105 Conditional sentences,

present unreal 2

Write the correct form of the verb in order to complete the present unreal conditional sentences below.

1. If Marcia studied harder, she (pass) her examinations easily.   *would pass*

2. If I knew how to play the piano, I (play) for my friends every night.   _____

3. If I didn't have to work today, I (go) swimming in our pool.   _____

4. If Tom had more practice in conversation, he (speak) English much better.   _____

5. If she knew how to drive well, she (have) fewer accidents.   _____

6. If I liked languages better, I (study) French as well as English.   _____

7. If Randy had the time, he (go) to Mexico with us.   _____

8. If she spent more time on her homework, she (get) better grades.   _____

9. If we studied together, we (make) more progress.   _____

10. If I had an automobile, I (take) a trip to Miami.   _____

11. If it didn't cost so much, I (go) to Europe by plane.   _____

12. If I didn't live so far away, I (walk) to school every day.   _____

13. If I had the money, I (buy) some new clothes.   _____

14. If I knew her better, I (ask) her to go with us.   _____

15. If I had the money, I (give) it to you gladly.   _____

16. If I had a good book to read, I (stay) at home tonight and read.   _____

17. If we left right away, we (be) there by two o'clock.   _____

18. If I took the noon train, I (get) there by two o'clock.   _____

present unreal 3

Dependent clauses of present unreal conditional sentences use the past tense form of all verbs *except* to be. To be *takes the special form* were *in all persons in these clauses.*

> If he *were* smart, he wouldn't say a word.
>
> If I *were* in your place, I would not argue with the police officer.

Write the correct form of the verb in order to complete the present unreal conditional sentences below.

1. If I (be) in your position, I would not go with him.   *were*
2. If today (be) Saturday, I would not have to work.   _____
3. If the weather (be) warmer, we could go to the beach.   _____
4. If he (be) a friend of mine, I would ask him about it.   _____
5. If I (be) not so busy today, I would go fishing with you.   _____
6. If I (be) a millionaire, I would spend every winter in Miami.   _____
7. If Alan (be) here now, we could ask him about it.   _____
8. If Sue (be) more intelligent, she would never say such a thing.   _____
9. If I (be) not so tired tonight, I would go to the movies with you.   _____
10. If today (be) a holiday, we could all go on a picnic.   _____
11. If I were you, I (explain) everything to him.   _____
12. If Patricia were only here now, she (know) how to handle this matter.   _____
13. If today were a holiday, we (go) to the beach.   _____
14. If I were not so busy, I (go) with you.   _____
15. If you were a millionaire, you (travel) a lot.   _____
16. If she were more ambitious, she (not be) content with such a low-paying job.   _____
17. If I were in your position, I (continue) to study English for several years more.   _____
18. If she were my boss, I (ask) her for a raise.   _____

past unreal 1

In past unreal conditional sentences, the dependent clause is in the past perfect tense, and the main clause uses would have, should have, could have, or might have. *The contracted forms (I'd, wouldn't have, etc.) are generally used.*

> If you *had studied*, you *would have passed* the exam.
>
> If you *had studied*, you'd *have passed* the exam.
>
> If I *had known*, I *wouldn't have said* anything.

Write the correct form of the verb in order to complete the past unreal conditional sentences below.

1. If he (study) more, he would have passed his examination.   *had studied*

2. If I (know) you were waiting for me, I would have hurried to get here.   _____

3. If you (telephone) me, I would have waited for you.   _____

4. If the weather yesterday (be) nice, we would have gone to the beach.   _____

5. If yesterday (be) a holiday, the stores would all have been closed.   _____

6. If you (go) with us, you would have seen a good show.   _____

7. If she (tell) me the truth, I would have been less angry.   _____

8. If I (receive) an invitation, I would have gone with you to the party.   _____

9. If he (had) enough money, he would have bought a new car.   _____

10. If I (think) about it in time, I would have asked Giselle to go with us.   _____

11. If I (see) him, I would have given him your message.   _____

12. If it (not rain) so hard, we would have been able to make the trip.   _____

13. If she (leave) in time, she would have caught the train.   _____

14. If I (take) a taxi, I would not have missed him.   _____

15. If you (telephone) me, I would have been glad to go with you.   _____

16. If I (know) about this yesterday, I could have brought the money with me.   _____

past unreal 2

Write the correct form of the verb in order to complete the past unreal conditional sentences below. Use contractions where appropriate.

1. If Saul had studied harder, he (pass) his examinations.   *would have passed*

2. If I had had your telephone number, I (call) you.   _____

3. If yesterday had been a holiday, we (go) to the beach.   _____

4. If I had known about this last night, I (act) differently.   _____

5. If he had attended class more regularly, he (get) a better grade.   _____

6. If they had left earlier, they (catch) the train.   _____

7. If I had been in your place, I (refuse) to give him the money.   _____

8. If I had seen her, I (give) her your message.   _____

9. If they had come on time, I (talk) with them.   _____

10. If she had had more experience, she (get) the job.   _____

11. If she had paid more attention in class, she (do) better on her examination.   _____

12. If they had invited me, I (go) with them.   _____

13. If I had had the money, I (buy) that car.   _____

14. If she had acted differently, we (take) her along.   _____

15. If I had been in your position, I (go) with them.   _____

16. If you had gone with us, you (meet) her.   _____

17. If I had had a car last summer, I (drive) to California.   _____

18. If it had not rained, we (go) on a picnic yesterday.   _____

19. If you had come earlier, you (have) a fine dinner.   _____

20. If she had told me the truth, I (be) less angry.   _____

21. If I had known it was going to rain, I (take) my umbrella.   _____

22. If we had hurried, we (get) there in time.   _____

109 *Wish*

Wish *suggests a situation that is unreal. After* wish, *use a past tense clause to suggest present action and a past perfect tense clause to suggest past action.*

> I *wish* I *knew* what to do in this situation. (present)
> I *wish* I *had known* what to do in that situation. (past)

Write the correct form of the verb in parentheses.

1. I wish I (know) how to swim.   *knew*
2. I wish I (go) with you to the opera last night. _____
3. Vanessa wishes she (speak) Dutch. _____
4. I wish I (have) an automobile. _____
5. I wish you (telephone) me yesterday about this. _____
6. I wish I (study) last night. _____
7. Harry wishes he (be) in his native country now. _____
8. I wish I (be) in Florida during this cold spell. _____
9. I wish today (be) Sunday. _____
10. I wish I (know) that you were going to the beach yesterday. _____
11. I wish I (start) to study English long ago. _____
12. I wish I (study) English with Michelle last year. _____
13. I wish I (know) English perfectly. _____
14. Kathy wishes she (have) today off. _____
15. Peter wishes he (be) an engineer instead of a doctor. _____
16. I wish I (have) today off. I would go swimming. _____
17. I wish I (have) yesterday off. I would have gone swimming. _____
18. I wish today (be) Saturday. I would not have to work, and I could go to the beach. _____
19. I wish yesterday (be) Saturday. I would not have had to work, and I could have gone to the beach. _____
20. I wish the weather (be) warm so that we could go to the park. _____

110 Present tense with future
clauses

When a dependent clause introduced by if **describes a future possibility, it uses the present tense. When dependent clauses introduced by** as long as, as soon as, before, unless, until, when, **and** while **describe a future condition, they also use the present tense.**

> I'll see him *when* he *comes.*
> I'll see him *as soon as* he *comes.*
> I'll wait for him *until* he *arrives.*
> *While I'm* at the supermarket, I'll pick up a pasta salad.

Write the correct form of the verbs in parentheses.

1. I will see him as soon as he (get) here.   *gets*
2. I will give it to her when she (arrive).   _____
3. Before I (leave), I will explain everything to him.   _____
4. We will leave as soon as Anita (get) here.   _____
5. Do not leave until I (let) you know.   _____
6. I won't go unless you (go), too.   _____
7. Wait right here until I (telephone) you.   _____
8. I'll let you know as soon as I (get) back.   _____
9. Don't call unless you (need) me badly.   _____
10. We will have to wait here until the doctor (arrive).   _____
11. Keep an eye on my bag while I (get) my ticket.   _____
12. When the weather (get) warmer, you can go swimming.   _____
13. Give him my message as soon as you (see) him.   _____
14. Don't leave until Olga (get) back.   _____
15. Wait right here while I (telephone).   _____
16. I must wait here until the mail (arrive).   _____
17. Call me as soon as you (hear) from them.   _____
18. Wait here until Ted (come).   _____
19. We can tell her when she (return) from her trip.   _____
20. The program won't begin until the president (arrive).   _____

111 Homophones

Homophones are words that have the same pronunciation but which differ in meaning. Write the corresponding homophone for each of the words listed.

1.	their	*there*	26.	seem	_____
2.	weight	*wait*	27.	some	_____
3.	threw	_____	28.	hole	_____
4.	knew	_____	29.	higher	_____
5.	waist	_____	30.	him	_____
6.	way	_____	31.	meet	_____
7.	weak	_____	32.	made	_____
8.	wood	_____	33.	mail	_____
9.	knight	_____	34.	in	_____
10.	know	_____	35.	clothes	_____
11.	cell	_____	36.	our	_____
12.	cellar	_____	37.	break	_____
13.	cent	_____	38.	knot	_____
14.	scene	_____	39.	pear	_____
15.	forth	_____	40.	plane	_____
16.	die	_____	41.	piece	_____
17.	flour	_____	42.	buy	_____
18.	road	_____	43.	role	_____
19.	right	_____	44.	guessed	_____
20.	red	_____	45.	steal	_____
21.	sail	_____	46.	so	_____
22.	sees	_____	47.	son	_____
23.	berth	_____	48.	principle	_____
24.	heal	_____	49.	pail	_____
25.	hear	_____	50.	dear	_____

112 Vocabulary review:

opposites from prefixes

Many words form their opposites by taking a prefix. Write the opposites of the words listed by adding the necessary prefixes.

1. happy	*unhappy*	25. fortunate _____
2. legal	*illegal*	26. fair _____
3. able	_____	27. (to) agree _____
4. believable	_____	28. (to) approve _____
5. regular	_____	29. polite _____
6. honest	_____	30. discreet _____
7. (to) appear	_____	31. correct _____
8. (to) obey	_____	32. sincere _____
9. (to) like	_____	34. furnished _____
11. legible	_____	35. healthy _____
12. (to) pronounce	_____	36. opened _____
13. (to) connect	_____	37. armed _____
14. (to) continue	_____	38. patient _____
15. (to) understand	_____	39. accurate _____
16. (to) tie	_____	40. (to) infect _____
17. (to) wrap	_____	41. (to) inherit _____
18. (to) button	_____	42. convenient _____
19. advantage	_____	43. real _____
20. mature	_____	44. kind _____
21. capable	_____	45. satisfied _____
22. organized	_____	46. agreeable _____
23. (to) dress	_____	47. pleasant _____
24. (to) fold	_____	48. dependent _____

Write the correct prepositions or particles in the blanks.

1. The boys in the class like to play tricks _____ Tom.   *on*

2. She never pays any attention _____ what the teacher says.   _____

3. I think that he has fallen _____ love with Annie.   _____

4. The senator insisted that he had had nothing to do _____ the scandal.   _____

5. I see Jack once _____ a while in the school cafeteria.   _____

6. I know several of Frost's poems _____ heart.   _____

7. It took me several weeks to get rid _____ my cold.   _____

8. I want to pick _____ a present to give to Sue for her birthday.   _____

9. I feel sorry _____ anyone who is as poor as he is.   _____

10. Let's go _____ a movie. I don't feel like studying.   _____

11. We are looking forward _____ her visit.   _____

12. Peter insisted _____ helping me with my homework.   _____

13. Because of his dark hair and eyes, everyone always takes Sam _____ my brother. _____

14. I refuse to put up _____ his actions any longer.   _____

15. During our telephone conversation, Pam became angry and hung up _____ me.   _____

16. The teacher always stands _____ front of the class.   _____

17. New York City is the largest city _____ the United States.   _____

18. My book is different _____ yours.   _____

19. Sally has been a teacher in this school _____ 1982.   _____

20. He has tried several times to borrow money _____ me.   _____

21. When are you going _____ vacation?   _____

Select the correct answer and write it in the space provided.

1. To *drop someone a line* is to (telephone, write, visit, save) him or her.   *write*

2. The opposite of *sharp* is (broad, cute, dull, frequent).   _____

3. Someone who is *punctual* always (arrives late, arrives on time, comes empty-handed, needs money).   _____

4. What is the corresponding noun form of the verb *to widen?*   _____

5. What is the corresponding noun form of the verb *to paralyze?*   _____

6. What is the corresponding adjective form of the noun *truth?*   _____

7. What is the corresponding adjective form of the noun *silence?*   _____

8. Someone who is *hard of hearing* is (difficult to hear, difficult to locate, partially deaf, soft-spoken).   _____

9. Which of these is a past participle: grow, draw, went, taken, saw?   _____

10. Which of these verbs has the same form in the past tense as in the present tense: bring, sing, bend, break, let?   _____

11. In which of the following words is the final letter *s* pronounced like *z:* takes, puts, bakes, comes, laughs?   _____

12. A common synonym for *seldom* is (often, usually, frequently, rarely).   _____

13. We pronounce the contraction *I'd* to rhyme with (lid, lied, led, lad).   _____

14. Which one of these words is not spelled correctly (whisper, testimoney, fastened, tremble, February)?   _____

15. We pronounce the word *touch* to rhyme with *couch, push, much, cough, rush).*   _____

16. *If someone* gives himself up, he (faints, falls down, gains courage, surrenders).   _____

17. *In vain* means (rapidly, often, without effective result, continuously).   _____

Select the correct form. Write your answers in the blanks.

1. He (said, told) me that his last name was Ortega. **told**

2. He asked me where (was I, I was) going. _____

3. Ronald said that he (will, would) be here before noon. _____

4. You ought (to do, to have done) this work yesterday. _____

5. If I (was, were) you, I would not mention it to him. _____

6. Call me as soon as Alice (arrives, will arrive). _____

7. If I (saw, had seen) Rose yesterday, I would have given her your message. _____

8. She wants to know where (do you live, you live). _____

9. We are old friends of (them, theirs, their). _____

10. This merchandise was supposed (to deliver, to have been delivered) yesterday. _____

11. Listen! I think the telephone (rings, is ringing). _____

12. Do you mind (to come, coming) back a little later? _____

13. He insisted (on waiting, to wait) for me after the lesson. _____

14. We had difficulty (in locating, to locate) him. _____

15. The train (supposed, is supposed) to arrive at two o'clock. _____

16. How long (do you study, have you studied) English? _____

17. We have been friends (during, for) many years. _____

18. Joan speaks Spanish (good, well). _____

19. He is (a, an) very honest man. _____

20. This is (a, an) easy exercise. _____

21. They (live, have lived) in that house for many years. _____

22. Ana always (comes, is coming) to school by bus. _____

23. When you telephoned, I (slept, was sleeping). _____

24. You (should telephone, should have telephoned) me last night. _____

116 Abbreviated clauses with *too*

We avoid repeating earlier words and phrases in English by using an appropriate auxiliary verb and too **in short affirmative clauses.**

> Henry went to the movies, and I went to the movies.
> Henry went to the movies, and I *did, too.*
> I like New York, and Alice likes New York.
> I like New York, and Alice *does, too.*

Rewrite the words in italics by using the correct auxiliary and too.

1. She studied English, and *I studied English.*   *did, too*

2. She is going to New York, and *he is going to New York.* _____

3. He knows Mr. Lee well, and *I know Mr. Lee well.* _____

4. He used to live in Washington, and *his brother used to live in Washington.* _____

5. I speak Spanish, and *she speaks Spanish.* _____

6. She will be at the meeting, and *I will be at the meeting.* _____

7. I had to work last night, and *Ed had to work last night.* _____

8. I have seen that picture, and *she has seen that picture.* _____

9. She saw the accident, and *I saw the accident.* _____

10. He was absent from the lesson, and *his sister was absent from the lesson.* _____

11. We enjoyed the concert, and *they enjoyed the concert.* _____

12. He is supposed to work tomorrow, and *I am supposed to work tomorrow.* _____

13. She can speak French, and *he can speak French.* _____

14. Tony has gone to the movies, and *Ann has gone to the movies.* _____

15. He is making good progress, and *she is making good progress.* _____

16. Sean likes to play tennis, and *I like to play tennis.* _____

17. He studies hard, and *his sister studies hard.* _____

18. You will be late, and *I will be late.* _____

19 He walks slowly, and *you walk slowly.* _____

20. She may go, and *I may go.* _____

We can also avoid repeating earlier words and phrases by using an appropriate auxiliary verb and so. **Note in the example that when we use** so, **the auxiliary precedes the subject.**

> Henry went to the movies, and I went to the movies.
> Henry went to the movies, and *so did I.*
> I like New York, and Alice likes New York.
> I like New York, and *so does Alice.*

Rewrite the words in italics by using the correct auxiliary and so.

1. *She studied English, and* I studied English.   *so did I*
2. You will be late, and *she will be late.* _____
3. They have seen that movie, and *I have seen that movie.* _____
4. He knows her well, and *I know her well.* _____
5. He can swim well, and *she can swim well.* _____
6. He wanted to go there, and *I wanted to go there.* _____
7. Penny will be absent from class, and *Gloria will be absent from class.* _____
8. I saw the accident, and *my wife saw the accident.* _____
9. She has many friends, and *her husband has many friends.* _____
10. Tom was arrested, and *his accomplice was arrested.* _____
11. He arrived late, and *I arrived late.* _____
12. She likes to watch television, and *her husband likes to watch television.* _____
13. They enjoyed the show, and *we enjoyed the show.* _____
14. The meat was salty, and *the vegetables were salty.* _____
15. I had to get up early, and *my wife had to get up early.* _____
16. We'll be here tomorrow, and *Josie will be here tomorrow.* _____
17. He would like to see the movie, and *I would like to see that movie.* _____
18. Your watch is fast, and *my watch is fast.* _____
19. She is studying French, and *her husband is studying French.* _____
20. He promised to come, and *his sister promised to come.* _____

either and *neither* 1

We use either **and** neither **to avoid repetition in negative sentences.**

> He doesn't like jazz, and she doesn't like jazz.
> He doesn't like jazz, and she *doesn't either.*
> He doesn't like jazz, and *neither does she.*
> Susan didn't go to the concert, and I didn't go to the concert.
> Susan didn't go to the concert, and I *didn't either.*
> Susan didn't go to the concert, and *neither did I.*

Rewrite the words in italics by using the correct auxiliary and either.

1. She didn't like the movie, and *I didn't like the movie.*   *I didn't, either*
2. We won't be there, and *Louise won't be there.* _____
3. He doesn't study much, and *she doesn't study much.* _____
4. Edna is not going to the party, and *I am not going to the party.* _____
5. I don't like the climate there, and my *wife doesn't like the climate there.* _____
6. Debbie won't be able to go, and *I won't be able to go.* _____
7. I didn't see the accident, and *Dick didn't see the accident.* _____
8. You won't like that picture, and *your wife won't like that picture.* _____
9. I haven't seen that movie, and *Molly hasn't seen that movie.* _____
10. He didn't arrive on time, and *we didn't arrive on time.* _____
11. She doesn't have many friends, and *he doesn't have many friends.* _____
12. Angie can't go, and *I can't go.* _____
13. Ralph didn't see me, and *the teacher didn't see me.* _____
14. I'm not sorry about it, and *Grace isn't sorry about it.* _____
15. You can't blame me for that mistake, and *George can't blame me for that mistake.* _____
16. My watch doesn't run well, and *your watch doesn't run well.* _____
17. I didn't remember his name, and *Henry didn't remember his name.* _____

119 Abbreviated clauses with

either and *neither* 2

Rewrite the words in italics by using the correct auxiliary and neither.

1. She didn't like the concert, and *I didn't like the concert.*   *neither did I*

2. He didn't hear me, and *the teacher didn't hear me.*   _____

3. I can't speak Spanish, and *my wife can't speak Spanish.*   _____

4. He hasn't read the book, and *I haven't read the book.*   _____

5. They didn't enjoy the novel, and *we didn't enjoy the novel.*   _____

6. I couldn't hear him well, and *my companion couldn't hear him well.*   _____

7. We don't have a television set, and *they don't have a television set.*   _____

8. Cecile can't go, and *Gail can't go.*   _____

9. She hasn't said anything about it, and *I haven't said anything about it.*   _____

10. I won't be at the meeting, and *George won't be at the meeting.*   _____

11. I didn't hear anyone in the room, and *my wife didn't hear anyone in the room.*   _____

12. He hasn't prepared his homework, and *I haven't prepared my homework.*   _____

13. Your answer isn't correct, and *my answer isn't correct.*   _____

14. He doesn't eat lunch there, and *his friends don't eat lunch there.*   _____

15. Gertrude isn't going to the party, and *I'm not going to the party.*   _____

16. He didn't have any money with him, and *I didn't have any money with me.*   _____

17. Pete can't go with us, and *Rodney can't go with us.*   _____

18. You won't enjoy that show, and *your wife won't enjoy that show.*   _____

120 Abbreviated clauses

with auxiliary verbs

In sentences where we have two conflicting ideas, we avoid repetition of words and phrases by using but *and an appropriate auxiliary.*

> They can't speak French. We can speak French.
> They can't speak French, *but we can.*
> I like to ski. Harvey and Lisa don't like to ski.
> I like to ski, *but* Harvey and Lisa *don't.*

Use the correct auxiliary to complete the sentences below. Where there are negatives, use contractions.

1. He won't be able to go, but I _____.   *will*
2. She will arrive on time, but we _____.   _____
3. I liked the movie, but my wife _____.   _____
4. Robin is going to the party, but I _____.   _____
5. She knows him well, but I _____.   _____
6. She doesn't know her lesson well, but I _____.   _____
7. I prepared my lesson, but she _____.   _____
8. He arrived on time, but his wife _____.   _____
9. She won't lend you any money, but I _____.   _____
10. Henry has seen that movie, but I _____.   _____
11. I have never been to Europe, but my wife _____.   _____
12. Alex can speak English, but his sons _____.   _____
13. Grace came home for lunch, but Helen _____.   _____
14. She plays the piano well, but her sister _____.   _____
15. My wife doesn't want to go to the concert, but I _____.   _____
16. She enjoys living in the north, but her husband _____.   _____
17. Murray isn't going to the beach, but I _____.   _____
18. At first, I didn't like living in New York, but now I _____.   _____
19. She says she knows him well, but I don't think she _____.   _____
20. They don't have class tomorrow, but we _____.   _____

and adjective forms 1

Write the noun form which corresponds to each of the adjectives listed.

1.	curious	*curiosity*	26.	ignorant	_____
2.	innocent	*innocence*	27.	emphatic	_____
3.	proud	_____	28.	strange	_____
4.	sick	_____	29.	happy	_____
5.	different	_____	30.	free	_____
6.	simple	_____	31.	weak	_____
7.	foolish	_____	32.	ill	_____
8.	young	_____	33.	sympathetic	_____
9.	sad	_____	34.	dangerous	_____
10.	important	_____	35.	dignified	_____
11.	difficult	_____	36.	absent	_____
12.	angry	_____	37.	kind	_____
13.	deep	_____	38.	religious	_____
14.	strong	_____	39.	true	_____
15.	high	_____	40.	silent	_____
16.	nervous	_____	41.	intelligent	_____
17.	dead	_____	42.	generous	_____
18.	beautiful	_____	43.	jealous	_____
19.	convenient	_____	44.	cruel	_____
20.	ugly	_____	45.	confident	_____
21.	gentle	_____	46.	wealthy	_____
22.	bitter	_____	47.	healthy	_____
23.	possible	_____	48.	anxious	_____
24.	wide	_____	49.	mysterious	_____
25.	sarcastic	_____	50.	noisy	_____

and adjective forms 2

Write the adjective form which corresponds to each of the nouns listed.

1.	success	*successful*	25.	religion	_____
2.	enthusiasm	*enthusiastic*	26.	ignorance	_____
3.	advantage	_____	27.	noise	_____
4.	sarcasm	_____	28.	truth	_____
5.	anger	_____	29.	ambition	_____
6.	fortune	_____	30.	power	_____
7.	humor	_____	31.	silence	_____
8.	dignity	_____	32.	importance	_____
9.	mercy	_____	33.	depth	_____
10.	patience	_____	34.	height	_____
11.	energy	_____	35.	width	_____
12.	dirt	_____	36.	length	_____
13.	absence	_____	37.	strength	_____
14.	necessity	_____	38.	cruelty	_____
15.	beauty	_____	39.	intelligence	_____
16.	disgrace	_____	40.	presence	_____
17.	rain	_____	41.	generosity	_____
18.	wave	_____	42.	bitterness	_____
19.	affection	_____	43.	death	_____
20.	mystery	_____	44.	freedom	_____
21.	suspicion	_____	45.	simplicity	_____
22.	style	_____	46.	confusion	_____
23.	pride	_____	47.	indifference	_____
24.	sentiment	_____	48.	regularity	_____

123 Perfect form of infinitives

The perfect form of the infinitive is used to describe an action that happened before the time of the main verb of the sentence. Form the perfect form of the infinitive with have *and the past participle of the principal verb.*

> I am glad *to have met* you.
>
> We were sorry not *to have gone* to the play while it was in town.
>
> You are smart *to have bought* your winter clothes during the sale.

Write the infinitives in the perfect form. Note how the idea of the action taking place before the time of the main verb is evident.

1. I am sorry *to tell* you this.   *to have told*

2. He is thought *to be* the best person for the job. _____

3. You are lucky *to have* so many good friends. _____

4. I am sorry *to miss* such an important meeting. _____

5. It is a pleasure *to work* for him. _____

6. I am glad *to meet* you. _____

7. I am happy *to know* you. _____

8. It is an honor *to know* such a distinguished woman. _____

9. You are wise *to do* that right away. _____

10. I am glad *to see* you again. _____

11. He is lucky *to have* you as a friend. _____

12. She is said *to be* the strongest person in the government. _____

13. The train is supposed *to arrive* at five o'clock. _____

14. You ought *to do* this right away. _____

15. You are very wise *to save* your money. _____

16. She is lucky *to know* about this beforehand. _____

17. I am sorry not *to be able* to talk with her. _____

18. She seems *to like* him a lot. _____

19. They ought *to deliver* this immediately. _____

20. You were wrong *to show* him so little respect. _____

124 Must have, may have

Must have *shows a strong probability that something happened in the past. It is followed by the past participle.*

> By the looks of the street, it *must have rained* while we were in the movie theater.

May have *expresses a possibility that something happened in the past. It is also followed by the past participle.*

> They *may have gone* home already. I don't see them here.

A. In these sentences, write the past perfect form of must.

1. I cannot find my book. I (leave) it at home.   *must have left*

2. You (come) here by taxi.   _____

3. He speaks English so well that he (live) in England for many years.   _____

4. Gail (leave) home during the morning because she was not there when I telephoned at noon.   _____

5. I imagine, from things they have told me, that they (be) very wealthy at one time.   _____

6. Paula (study) very hard before her examination.   _____

7. She (be) a very smart woman when she was younger.   _____

8. You (work) very fast in order to have finished that work so quickly.   _____

B. In these sentences, write the past perfect form of may.

1. I haven't any idea where Joy is. She (go) to the movies with Tim.   *may have gone*

2. The bad weather (delay) them.   _____

3. You (lost) your keys on the bus.   _____

4. It's strange Joe is not here for his appointment, but he (forget) all about it.   _____

5. One of the strangers (steal) the money.   _____

6. Al (take) your book by mistake.   _____

7. They (telephone) while we were out.   _____

8. They (be) wealthy at one time, but I doubt it.   _____

conditional sentences

Write the correct form of the verb in the conditional sentences below.

1. If I had known about this yesterday,
   I (help) him.   *would have helped*

2. If I (be) you, I would not mention it to him. _____

3. I would have gone if I (have) the time. _____

4. If I see her, I (give) her your message. _____

5. If he had been driving fast, everyone (kill). _____

6. If I could help you, I (do) so gladly. _____

7. If the weather were warm today, we (go)
   to the beach. _____

8. If the weather had been warm yesterday, we (go)
   to the beach. _____

9. If I (see) Rose, I will tell her the good news. _____

10. If we decide to go, we (let) you know. _____

11. I would have bought the car if I (have) the money. _____

12. He will pass his examinations if he (study) hard. _____

13. He would pass his examinations if he (study) hard. _____

14. He would have passed his examinations
    if he (study) hard. _____

15. If I took the noon train, I (arrive)
    in New Orleans at nine. _____

16. I would certainly have given her the message
    if I (see) her. _____

17. If it were not raining, I (work) in my garden. _____

18. If I (have) your telephone number,
    I would have called you. _____

19. Joan would have gone with us if she (not be) ill. _____

20. If Ana had been with us, the accident (not happen). _____

21. Perhaps the man would not have died if there
    (be) a doctor present. _____

22. If I were a millionaire, I (spend) all my winters
    in Florida. _____

Change the following sentences to the negative form.

1. She speaks English well.   *does not speak*
2. We went to the movies last night.   _____
3. She ought to tell him about it.   _____
4. He should have told her about it.   _____
5. He has lived there for many years.   _____
6. They were supposed to arrive yesterday.   _____
7. She can speak Spanish perfectly.   _____
8. She will return at five o'clock.   _____
9. He had to work late last night.   _____
10. He has three brothers.   _____
11. She is the best student in our class.   _____
12. You may smoke here.   _____
13. There were many students absent from class today.   _____
14. They were driving very fast at the time.   _____
15. I would like to have that kind of job.   _____
16. They go to the beach on Sunday.   _____
17. She knows him well.   _____
18. They got married in June.   _____
19. We should lend him more money.   _____
20. We arrived at the theater on time.   _____
21. She listens to her mother.   _____
22. They will go without us.   _____
23. He smokes a lot.   _____
24. He has been studying English a long time.   _____

Answer Key

Exercise 1

2. his	6. its	10. her	14. their	18. your
3. our	7. Her	11. our	15. their	19. her
4. their	8. your	12. his	16. her	20. his
5. her	9. my	13. my	17. its	21. his

Exercise 2

2. us	6. its	10. it	14. it	18. her
3. them	7. them	11. her	15. them	19. him
4. them	8. it	12. it	16. him/her	20. it
5. you	9. them	13. them	17. us	21. them

Exercise 3

2. myself	6. myself	10. themselves	14. himself
3. himself	7. itself	11. himself/herself	15. yourself
4. ourselves	8. herself	12. myself	16. himself
5. themselves	9. ourselves	13. himself	17. myself

Exercise 4

2. theirs	6. his	10. mine	14. yours	18. yours
3. mine	7. yours	11. theirs	15. yours	19. theirs
4. his	8. yours	12. ours	16. hers	20. hers
5. ours	9. hers	13. mine	17. his	21. his

Exercise 5

2. ties	11. oxen	20. tails	29. cars	38. cousins
3. classes	12. pencils	21. women	30. covers	39. pens
4. teachers	13. cafeterias	22. brothers	31. buses	40. sisters
5. beaches	14. students	23. notebooks	32. feet	41. matches
6. windows	15. wishes	24. hands	33. dishes	42. coats
7. doors	16. headaches	25. mice	34. men	43. cats
8. dresses	17. boxes	26. hats	35. kisses	44. noses
9. watches	18. schools	27. geese	36. faces	
10. books	19. children	28. losses	37. churches	

Exercise 6

2. dishes	9. classes	16. keys	23. leaves	30. lunches
3. children	10. buses	17. churches	24. dresses	31. feet
4. cities	11. streets	18. heroes	25. sisters	32. pillows
5. books	12. exercises	19. women	26. matches	33. companies
6. knives	13. wishes	20. armies	27. letters	34. ladies
7. boxes	14. copies	21. halves	28. hats	35. mice
8. potatoes	15. pens	22. brothers	29. men	36. wives

Exercise 7

2. likes	10. tries	18. leaves	26. cries	34. uses
3. plays	11. speaks	19. sits	27. pays	35. passes
4. goes	12. notices	20. knows	28. sings	36. cashes
5. carries	13. says	21. thinks	29. wishes	37. fixes
6. teaches	14. passes	22. sees	30. pushes	38. replies
7. shows	15. washes	23. laughs	31. pulls	
8. does	16. catches	24. matches	32. dresses	
9. watches	17. brings	25. dances	33. misses	

Exercise 8

3. She must go	17. She can wait	31. She wishes
4. She is	18. She waits	32. She can meet
5. She has	19. She is waiting	33. She tries
6. She will see	20. She will wait	34. She is leaving
7. She may study	21. She has waited	35. She uses
8. She has seen	22. She likes	36. She washes
9. She is studying	23. She must see	37. She is going
10. She will be	24. She has been	38. She will know
11. She can go	25. She will take	39. She must try
12. She should study	26. She is working	40. She has tried
13. She plays	27. She may work	41. She will try
14. She carries	28. She works	42. She ought to see
15. She goes	29. She wants	
16. She ought to go	30. She does	

Exercise 9

2. has	6. are	10. listens	14. goes	18. are	22. is
3. study	7. explain	11. play	15. come	19. want	23. goes
4. studies	8. are	12. is	16. does	20. have	24. stays
5. are	9. watch	13. lives	17. makes	21. has	

Exercise 10

2. These are	10. These pencils belong	18. The buses are
3. We are	11. The tomatoes are	19. The men have left
4. They like	12. The dishes are	20. They will leave
5. Those books belong	13. The classes have started	21. They can speak
6. They were	14. The women are waiting	22. The boys must study
7. The boys do	15. These books are	23. They were
8. They are waiting	16. We are going to study	24. The leaves are falling
9. The children are	17. They are making	

Exercise 11

2. low	12. backward	22. pull	32. high	42. bad
3. depart	13. rude	23. narrow	33. over	43. winter
4. outside	14. thin	24. tight	34. west	44. little/small
5. domestic	15. after	25. dirty	35. south	45. lose
6. asleep	16. behind	26. present	36. early	46. forget
7. cowardly	17. cheap	27. ugly	37. sell	47. past
8. soft	18. wet	28. sad	38. short	48. worst
9. dull	19. true	29. difficult	39. seldom	
10. rough	20. parent	30. wide	40. sour	
11. lend	21. full	31. find	41. effect	

Exercise 12

2. with	7. from	12. at	17. at	22. to
3. in	8. for	13. for	18. about	23. for
4. by	9. in	14. in	19. for	24. by
5. to	10. around	15. for	20. on	
6. to	11. in	16. by	21. to	

Exercise 13

2. lately	7. at the point of doing	12. difficulty
3. laugh	8. talked	13. explanation
4. know	9. w	14. sneeze
5. telephone	10. h	15. the third
6. visit	11. excellent	16. at eight at the latest

Exercise 14

2. is running	8. either	14. wrote	20. an
3. have lived	9. anyone	15. makes	21. has
4. were	10. has worked	16. me to go	22. are there
5. me	11. comes	17. to learn	
6. are having	12. on	18. he lives	
7. many	13. get	19. These	

Exercise 15

2. forced	9. married	16. cried	23. spelled	30. supposed
3. studied	10. managed	17. seemed	24. faced	31. referred
4. indicated	11. carried	18. enjoyed	25. worried	32. insisted
5. needed	12. played	19. appeared	26. depended	33. noticed
6. learned	13. guided	20. helped	27. decreased	34. admitted
7. practiced	14. planned	21. traveled	28. remained	
8. used	15. hoped	22. pleased	29. pointed	

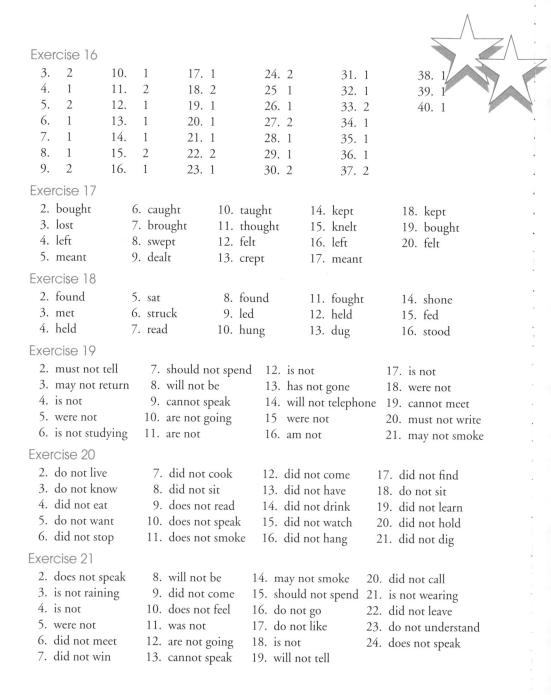

Exercise 16

3.	2	10.	1	17.	1	24.	2	31.	1	38.	1
4.	1	11.	2	18.	2	25	1	32.	1	39.	1
5.	2	12.	1	19.	1	26.	1	33.	2	40.	1
6.	1	13.	1	20.	1	27.	2	34.	1		
7.	1	14.	1	21.	1	28.	1	35.	1		
8.	1	15.	2	22.	2	29.	1	36.	1		
9.	2	16.	1	23.	1	30.	2	37.	2		

Exercise 17

2. bought	6. caught	10. taught	14. kept	18. kept
3. lost	7. brought	11. thought	15. knelt	19. bought
4. left	8. swept	12. felt	16. left	20. felt
5. meant	9. dealt	13. crept	17. meant	

Exercise 18

2. found	5. sat	8. found	11. fought	14. shone
3. met	6. struck	9. led	12. held	15. fed
4. held	7. read	10. hung	13. dug	16. stood

Exercise 19

2. must not tell	7. should not spend	12. is not	17. is not
3. may not return	8. will not be	13. has not gone	18. were not
4. is not	9. cannot speak	14. will not telephone	19. cannot meet
5. were not	10. are not going	15 were not	20. must not write
6. is not studying	11. are not	16. am not	21. may not smoke

Exercise 20

2. do not live	7. did not cook	12. did not come	17. did not find
3. do not know	8. did not sit	13. did not have	18. do not sit
4. did not eat	9. does not read	14. did not drink	19. did not learn
5. do not want	10. does not speak	15. did not watch	20. did not hold
6. did not stop	11. does not smoke	16. did not hang	21. did not dig

Exercise 21

2. does not speak	8. will not be	14. may not smoke	20. did not call
3. is not raining	9. did not come	15. should not spend	21. is not wearing
4. is not	10. does not feel	16. do not go	22. did not leave
5. were not	11. was not	17. do not like	23. do not understand
6. did not meet	12. are not going	18. is not	24. does not speak
7. did not win	13. cannot speak	19. will not tell	

Exercise 22

2. Can she speak
3. Is she
4. May he sit
5. Were they
6. Is she
7. Can he go
8. Should he mention
9. Will they be
10. Is she studying
11. Has Mr. Darbari gone
12. Will she telephone
13. Is he
14. Were there
15. Should he study
16. Are they
17. Were they
18. Is it raining
19. Are they going
20. Will she be

Exercise 23

2. Did they leave
3. Does she study
4. Did he buy
5. Does she drive
6. Did Daniela answer
7. Did he sit
8. Does he speak
9. Do they go
10. Did they meet
11. Did the child cut
12. Did she give
13. Do they live
14. Do you drink
15. Does the trolley come
16. Did the train arrive
17. Does he write
18. Did they bring
19. Did he lose
20. Did they catch
21. Does Valentina smoke

Exercise 24

2. Will he be
3. Is Harriet
4. Does he work
5. Did the boys spend
6. Does Paula play
7. Does his sister sing
8. Is the telephone ringing
9. Does it look
10. Do we have
11. Is the sun shining
12. Is the weather becoming
13. Did it rain
14. Can Loretta speak
15. Must he see
16. Will Antonia tell
17. Does the man speak
18. Could Beatrice understand
19. Did the train leave
20. Will it arrive
21. Does he have
22. Does she feel
23. Does he want
24. Did they spend

Exercise 25

3. _____
4. the
5. _____
6. The
7. _____
8. The
9. _____
10. _____
11. _____
12. The

Exercise 26

2. is ringing
3. writes
4. is writing
5. smokes
6. smokes
7. is smoking
8. rains
9. is beginning
10. is knocking
11. stops
12. is stopping
13. get
14. are building
15. have
16. are having
17. is waving
18. comes
19. is sleeping
20. sleeps
21. speaks

Exercise 27

2. were sitting
3. was shining
4. was walking
5. were having
6. was studying
7. was playing
8. were driving
9. was writing
10. was getting
11. was preparing
12. was having
13. was raining
14. was shining
15. was talking
16. were watching
17. was having
18. were sleeping
19. was suffering

Exercise 28

2. was sleeping
3. was blowing
4. rained
5. was raining
6. was playing
7. played
8. were having
9. read
10. was reading
11. wrote
12. was writing
13. was shining
14. was ringing
15. drove
16. was driving
17. played
18. was playing
19. saw
20. was leaving
21. waited
22. were waiting

Exercise 29

2. on
3. at
4. from
5. to
6. at
7. with
8. by
9. over
10. on
11. to
12. with
13. on
14. in
15. for
16. in
17. at
18. for
19. for
20. for
21. about
22. of
23. with
24. about
25. from

Exercise 30

2. literate
3. February
4. worst
5. best
6. did
7. will
8. have
9. danger
10. high
11. missed
12. l
13. giraffe
14. telephone
15. cancel
16. occasionally
17. take
18. pull
19. empty

Exercise 31

2. I lived
3. were
4. an
5. an
6. These
7. ran
8. could
9. smoke
10. is playing
11. for
12. saw
13. were eating
14. comes
15. her
16. is crossing
17. was raining
18. has worked
19. either
20. us to wait
21. were
22. seen

Exercise 32

2. has to go
3. has to leave
4. have to be
5. have to learn
6. have to have
7. has to work
8. has to go
9. have to wait
10. have to go
11. has to spend
12. have to go
13. has to be
14. have to leave
15. have to write
16. has to write
17. have to remain
18. have to get
19. has to remain
20. has to visit

Exercise 33

A.
2. had to leave
3. had to work
4. had to get up
5. had to walk
6. had to learn
7. had to have

B.
2. will have to return
3. will have to do
4. will have to be
5. will have to buy
6. will have to wait
7. will have to make

C.
2. has had to learn
3. have had to go
4. have had to return
5. have had to take
6. has had to cook
7. have had to buy

Exercise 34

2. didn't have to leave
3. don't have to study
4. don't have to write
5. didn't have to wait
6. doesn't have to spend
7. don't have to return
8. doesn't have to be
9. don't have to leave
10. didn't have to walk
11. won't have to send
12. don't have to wait
13. didn't have to pay
14. didn't have to go
15. don't have to cash
16. won't have to invite
17. doesn't have to take
18. didn't have to join
19. doesn't have to leave
20. don't have to write
21. didn't have to write

Exercise 35

2. Did he have to stay
3. Do the students have to learn
4. Will they have to write
5. Did she have to wait
6. Do you have to return
7. Did she have to go
8. Does she have to take
9. Did we have to invite
10. Does he have to leave
11. Will we have to write
12. Do they have to arrive
13. Does Tom have to get up
14. Does Sue have to help
15. Did she have to prepare
16. Does she have to work
17. Did they have to stay
18. Does he have to go
19. Do I have to sign
20. Did we have to send
21. Do we have to save

Exercise 36

2. said
3. said
4. said
5. told
6. told
7. said
8. said
9. tell
10. said
11. said
12. told
13. told
14. told

Exercise 37

2. lived
3. began
4. has studied
5. studied
6. began
7. lasted
8. were
9. have lived
10. had
11. have had
12. have been
13. became
14. has been

133

Exercise 38

2. one pound
3. one mile
4. seven ante meridiem
5. six post meridiem
6. six tenths
7. one half
8. one fourth/quarter
9. six percent
10. number five
11. sixty-eight degrees
12. alternating current
13. direct current
14. et cetera
15. one gallon
16. television
17. cash on delivery
18. quart
19. pint
20. yard
21. inch
22. and
23. Incorporated
24. two years
25. four feet
26. Nine-sixth Street
27. Avenue
28. Boulevard
29. Road
30. Building
31. February
32. August
33. December
34. square feet
35. first
36. third
37. seventh
38. Thursday
39. Wednesday
40. National Broadcasting Company
41. New York
42. California
43. Illinois
44. Washington
45. Connecticut
46. Ohio
47. Michigan
48. Tennessee

Exercise 39

2. have been living
3. have been trying
4. has been driving
5. has been feeling
6. has been sitting
7. has been working
8. have been talking
9. has been speaking
10. has been working
11. has been teaching
12. have been going
13. have been waiting
14. has been raining
15. have been whistling
16. has been studying
17. has been wearing
18. have been working
19. have been planning

Exercise 40

2. since
3. for
4. ago
5. for
6. for
7. since
8. since
9. for
10. since
11. ago
12. since
13. for
14. since
15. ago
16. since
17. for
18. since
19. ago
20. for

Exercise 41

2. had stolen
3. had taken
4. had had
5. had found
6. had seen
7. had left
8. had played
9. had left
10. had lived
11. had looked
12. had taken
13. had had
14. had received
15. had done
16. had put
17. had left
18. had broken

Exercise 42

2. did not leave
3. is not
4. did not want
5. has not studied
6. did not tell
7. will not return
8. is not having
9. have not left
10. cannot speak
11. must not tell
12. are not going
13. is not
14. was not
15. has not worked
16. have not been living
17. does not have to work
18. did not have to go
19. did not come
20. are not making
21. did not tell
22. does not prepare
23. were not playing
24. has not finished

Exercise 43

2. Did he give
3. Is she
4. Are we going
5. Will they return
6. Did he leave
7. Can Marcia swim
8. Is she going to study
9. Has he read
10. Has she been studying
11. Is she
12. Do we have to have
13. Did Robert have to leave
14. Will he return
15. Were they having
16. Did they build
17. Will they deliver
18. Was she
19. Is it
20. Is the wind blowing
21. Were there
22. Did the child cut
23. Did the boy run
24. Is the doorbell ringing

Exercise 44

2. of
3. about
4. up
5. at
6. about
7. on
8. at/about
9. about
10. for
11. since
12. over/above
13. below
14. in
15. on
16. out
17. with
18. in
19. from
20. in
21. in
22. from
23. in
24. to

Exercise 45

2. prefer to
3. entrance
4. agreement
5. explode
6. put
7. been
8. home
9. lacks
10. alone
11. in addition to
12. advice
13. seldom
14. recently
15. joking
16. w
17. t

Exercise 46

2. Washington, D.C.
3. five
4. one syllable
5. wild
6. vowel
7. first
8. regular
9. November
10. rises
11. two
12. sixteen
13. Thursday
14. north
15. have/has
16. winter
17. fifty-two
18. irregular
19. taken
20. twenty-six
21. longer
22. Civil War

Exercise 47

2. had seen
3. was reading
4. yours
5. had to
6. don't have to
7. were
8. were taking
9. needed
10. leave
11. is coming
12. are having
13. to us
14. me to go
15. me
16. blows
17. anyone
18. went
19. have been
20. said
21. are singing
22. an

Exercise 48

2. You're
3. She's
4. It's
5. She's
6. We're
7. They're
8. There's
9. You're
10. I'll
11. You'll
12. She'll
13. We'll
14. don't
15. doesn't
16. didn't
17. won't
18. won't
19. aren't
20. haven't

Exercise 49

2. for
3. for
4. to
5. for
6. for
7. to
8. to
9. for
10. to
11. to
12. for
13. to
14. to
15. to
16. to

Exercise 50

2. gave Antonia
3. sent him
4. show Rudy
5. paid the landlord
6. sold his friend
7. took her
8. brought me
9. bought her (his wife)
10. brought us
11. write you
12. gave her father
13. sent Ms. Pappas
14. told Sharon
15. gave each of us
16. lent his brother
17. hand me
18. sent each of them
19. gave Mike
20. send us
21. lent us
22. bring me

Exercise 51

2. flown
3. driven
4. broke
5. broken
6. fell
7. fallen
8. did
9. drew
10. gone
11. ate
12. froze
13. gave
14. chose
15. bitten
16. done

Exercise 52

2. is going to teach
3. are going to be
4. is going to meet
5. are going to stay
6. is going to go
7. is going to take
8. are going to go
9. is going to rain
10. are going to eat
11. is going to have
12. are going to go
13. is going to get married
14. are going to spend
15. is going to ask
16. are going to be
17. are going to go
18. are going to fly
19. is going to study

Exercise 53

2. was going to go
3. was going to study
4. were going to go
5. was going to call
6. was going to see
7. were going to buy
8. were going to visit
9. was going to be
10. were going to eat
11. was going to send
12. was going to lend
13. was going to let

Exercise 54

2. was
3. could
4. would
5. was
6. lived
7. was
8. liked
9. lived
10. could
11. would
12. might
13. was
14. had lost
15. meant
16. was
17. would
18. might
19. was
20. was

Exercise 55

3.	s	10.	s	17.	z	24.	z	31.	z	38.	z
4.	s	11.	z	18.	s	25.	z	32.	z	39.	s
5.	z	12.	s	19.	z	26.	s	33.	z	40.	z
6.	z	13.	s	20.	z	27.	z	34.	s	41.	z
7.	s	14.	z	21.	s	28.	z	35.	s	42.	z
8.	z	15.	s	22.	z	29.	s	36.	z	43.	s
9.	z	16.	z	23.	s	30.	s	37.	s	44.	z

Exercise 56

3.	t	10.	t	17.	d	24.	d	31.	d	38.	t
4.	t	11.	d	18.	d	25.	d	32.	d	39.	d
5.	d	12.	t	19.	t	26.	t	33.	t	40.	t
6.	t	13.	d	20.	d	27.	d	34.	d	41.	d
7.	t	14.	t	21.	d	28.	d	35.	t	42.	d
8.	d	15.	d	22.	d	29.	t	36.	d		
9.	t	16.	t	23.	t	30.	t	37.	t		

Exercise 57

2. get home
3. got in
4. gets ready
5. gets into
6. gets on
7. gets off
8. get very tired
9. got excited
10. get over
11. got into
12. get to
13. get home
14. get drunk
15. get married
16. get nervous

Exercise 58

3.	d	12.	g	21.	p	30.	c	39.	k	48.	h
4.	t	13.	b	22.	b	31.	b	40.	k	49.	c
5.	s	14.	t	23.	l	32.	g	41.	c	50.	b
6.	b	15.	l	24.	s	33.	b	42.	l		
7.	k	16.	l	25.	w	34.	w	43.	h		
8.	w, t	17.	l	26.	w	35.	w	44.	t		
9.	h	18.	k	27.	t	36.	t	45.	c		
10.	t	19.	k	28.	t	37.	w	46.	l		
11.	k	20.	d	29.	n	38.	b	47.	d		

Exercise 59

2. thin
3. get on
4. green
5. an adjective
6. twelfth
7. tight
8. dangerous
9. w
10. three
11. visit
12. west
13. west
14. vines
15. dozen
16. four
17. thirty-six
18. Ms.
19. nine
20. 1492
21. been
22. seen

Exercise 60

2. in/at	7. at	12. over	17. of	22. by
3. from	8. from	13. of	18. on	23. by
4. of	9. in	14. of	19. about	24. about
5. in	10. on	15. by	20. on	
6. after	11. off	16. out	21. in	

Exercise 61

2. on vines	6. camel	10. h	14. the second
3. breeze	7. apple pie	11. k	15. recently
4. recover from	8. bed	12. pointed	16. guarantee
5. success	9. asked	13. coach	17. gone

Exercise 62

2. had had	8. me to wait	14. is beginning	20. told
3. has saved	9. said	15. Not	21. could
4. were going	10. was	16. my name was	22. were having
5. went	11. would	17. a lot of	
6. whom	12. between	18. hers	
7. which	13. sits	19. mine	

Exercise 63

2. Many newspaper articles are written by her.
3. The room is cleaned by the maid every day.
4. Their quarrels are heard by everyone.
5. The mail is delivered by the letter carrier.
6. All the letters are written by the secretary.
7. Her speeches are enjoyed by everyone.
8. The magazine is sold by them everywhere.
9. Our exercises are corrected by her at home.
10. Dinner is prepared by Joe every night.
11. The mail is delivered by them at ten o'clock.
12. Urgent information is brought by a messenger.
13. The documents are signed by them in the attorney's office.
14. Presents were brought by her from Hong Kong.
15. Our compositions are corrected by the teacher.
16. The books are printed by them in Boston.
17. The grass is cut by him once a week.
18. The letters are sent by them by overnight mail.
19. The contracts are prepared by the lawyer.
20. The money is provided by the foundation.

Exercise 64

2. The money was taken by someone
3. The mail had been delivered by the letter carrier.
4. The letters have been signed by him.
5. Many books have been written by her.
6. The bills were paid by Marianne by check.
7. The work will be finished by them tomorrow.
8. The work had been finished by him in time.
9. The party has been planned by them.
10. Corn was grown by Native Americans in Mexico.
11. Several buildings have been designed by him.
12. The contract had been signed by him previously.
13. The plate was broken by her while she was washing it.
14. The accident was seen by Julia on her way home from work.
15. The tickets had been brought by them.
16. The child has been found by them at last.
17. The trees were planted by Sonia.
18. The dinner was prepared by them.
19. It will be sent by her immediately.
20. The key was used by him to open the door.

Exercise 65

2. It may be kept by the museum for two weeks.
3. The bill can be paid later.
4. It has to be delivered tomorrow.
5. Those things can't be put there.
6. It must be sent at once.
7. It should be delivered today.
8. It ought to be written now.
9. These exercises must be studied by Kevin.
10. It may be brought later.
11. This room can be used by Linda.
12. It has to be done soon.
13. He may be held by the police for several days.

Exercise 66

2. will not be delivered
3. must not be signed
4. was not shot
5. is not taught
6. was not wrapped
7. was not struck
8. has not been delivered
9. was not followed
10. were not heard
11. cannot be used
12. was not printed
13. were not sent
14. will not be delivered
15. cannot be sent
16. was not taken
17. were not disappointed
18. will not be prepared
19. has not been finished
20. had not been decorated

Exercise 67

2. Was the thief captured
3. Will the lecture be attended
4. Has the dinner been served
5. Are we invited
6. Will the work be done
7. Was the city destroyed
8. Must these letters be signed
9. Was America discovered
10. Has the house been struck
11. Was the tree blown
12. Were they arrested
13. Will his book be published
14. Must this project be finished
15. Is the mail delivered
16. Are the poems written
17. Was the car destroyed
18. Will their engagement be announced
19. Will they be married
20. Was the meeting held
21. Was it attended
22. Can all these books be borrowed

Exercise 68

2. _____
3. a
4. _____
5. _____
6. The
7. _____
8. The
9. the
10. an
11. _____
12. The
13. _____
14. The
15. The
16. a
17. a
18. _____
19. a
20. a
21. _____
22. The
23. the
24. _____
25. The

Exercise 69

2. torn
3. lain
4. known
5. shook
6. spoke
7. grown
8. threw
9. hid
10. worn
11. wrote
12. took
13. ridden
14. grew
15. seen
16. tore
17. spoken
18. knew
19. known
20. wore

Exercise 70

2. weak
3. no one
4. dead
5. true
6. rude
7. careless
8. start/begin
9. forget
10. right
11. late
12. always
13. fast
14. cause
15. rough
16. tighten
17. retail
18. cowardly
19. buy
20. noisy
21. wet
22. loose
23. backward
24. simple
25. full
26. sour
27. short
28. useful
29. decrease
30. lead
31. child
32. back
33. lower
34. comedy
35. different
36. west
37. fall
38. arrive
39. found
40. wild
41. absence
42. permanent
43. defeat
44. public
45. friend
46. borrow
47. add
48. innocent
49. rare
50. summer

Exercise 71

2. more intelligent than
3. earlier than
4. more interesting than
5. wider than
6. easier than
7. more beautifully than
8. faster than
9. sooner than
10. more clearly than
11. more often than
12. better than
13. colder than
14. busier than
15. harder than
16. more carefully than
17. more often than
18. earlier than
19. sweeter than
20. higher than

Exercise 72

2. as expensive as	8. as fast as	14. as hard as	20. as rich as
3. as old as	9. as soon as	15. as good as	21. as often as
4. as well as	10. as cold as	16. as often as	22. as soon as
5. as fast as	11. as quickly as	17. as rapidly as	
6. as soon as	12. as easily as	18. as carefully as	
7. as well as	13. as tired as	19. as beautifully as	

Exercise 73

2. somewhere	7. anything	12. someone	17. anyone
3. anyone	8. some	13. anyone	18. somewhere
4. any	9. somewhere	14. some	
5. some	10. any	15. anyone	
6. anyone	11. anything	16. any	

Exercise 74

2.	3	1st	8.	3	1st	14.	3	1st	20. 3 2nd
3.	5	3rd	9.	3	1st	15.	2	2nd	21. 3 2nd
4.	4	2nd	10.	3	1st	16.	4	3rd	22. 5 3rd
5.	4	2nd	11.	3	2nd	17.	3	2nd	23. 2 1st
6.	4	3rd	12.	2	2nd	18.	3	2nd	
7.	4	2nd	13.	5	4th	19.	2	2nd	

Exercise 75

2. had taken	10. took	18. is beginning
3. gets up	11. is sleeping	19. is crossing
4. saw	12. rises	20. arrive
5. have not seen	13. have not been	21. were running
6. has been	14. had seen	22. has taught/been teaching
7. lived	15. had not seen	23. will come
8. were (you) doing	16. were living	24. would come
9. is knocking	17. had discovered	25. will see

Exercise 76

2. twelve	10. north	18. one syllable
3. northeastern	11. Alaska	19. worst
4. Mississippi	12. Rhode Island	20. third
5. third	13. past participle	21. February
6. third	14. lay	22. George Washington
7. adverb	15. sat	
8. July 4	16. gone	
9. irregular	17. autumn (fall)	

Exercise 77

2. to	7. from	12. in	17. on	22. at
3. on	8. from	13. by	18. at	23. in
4. off	9. against	14. on	19. at	
5. for	10. on	15. for	20. on	
6. around	11. to	16. of	21. for	

Exercise 78

2. because of	6. enough	10. curious	14. pupil
3. sometimes	7. smooth	11. count	15. corporal
4. was	8. vines	12. razor	16. mice
5. rather good	9. explanation	13. heel	17. sheep

Exercise 79

2. was sleeping	8. could	14. were having	20. are having
3. go	9. anyone	15. said	21. have
4. has been	10. than	16. could	22. spent
5. mine	11. an	17. might	23. to us
6. us to wait	12. a	18. her	24. have been
7. is waiting	13. I lived	19. is coming	

Exercise 80

2. sang	6. begun	10. let	14. put	18. spread
3. rang	7. rung	11. sunk	15. swam	19. cost
4. set	8. hurt	12. shrank	16. cut	
5. put	9. drunk	13. sprang	17. hit	

Exercise 81

2. was supposed to leave	11. is supposed to be
3. am supposed to arrive	12. was supposed to leave
4. is supposed to be	13. were supposed to deliver
5. are supposed to go	14. was supposed to call
6. is supposed to bring	15. is supposed to be
7. was supposed to telephone	16. is supposed to leave
8. are supposed to write	17. is supposed to stay
9. is supposed to clean	18. were supposed to publish
10. was supposed to arrive	

Exercise 82

2. used to live	8. used to go	15. used to write
3. used to be	9. used to study	16. used to catch
4. used to walk	10. used to be	17. used to help
5. used to work	12. used to visit	18. used to dance
6. used to be	13. used to play	19. used to take
7. used to visit	14. used to send	20. used to walk

Exercise 83

2. Yes, it is.	No, it isn't.	9. Yes, we have.	No, we haven't.
3. Yes, it did.	No, it didn't.	10. Yes, I will.	No, I won't.
4. Yes, she is.	No, she isn't.	11. Yes, I am.	No, I'm not.
5. Yes, we have.	No, we haven't.	12. Yes, she does.	No, she doesn't.
6. Yes, she can.	No, she can't.	13. Yes, I was.	No, I wasn't.
7. Yes, it does.	No, it doesn't.	14. Yes, she was.	No, she wasn't.
8. Yes, he is.	No, he isn't.	15. Yes, he can.	No, he can't.

Exercise 84

2. isn't she	7. wasn't it	12. didn't you	17. won't you
3. aren't there	8. hasn't he	13. didn't I	18. wasn't it
4. didn't you	9. isn't he	14. isn't she	19. isn't he
5. won't it	10. isn't it	15. hasn't she	20. haven't you
6. can't she	11. doesn't it	16. isn't he	

Exercise 85

2. does it	7. have you	12. will she	17. was she
3. is he	8. did she	13. have you	18. has it
4. can she	9. can you	14. has it	19. has it
5. will you	10. do you	15. does it	20. will you
6. was it	11. does he	16. were you	

Exercise 86

2. is it	8. isn't she	14. doesn't she	20. didn't it
3. isn't he	9. won't you	15. haven't they	21. wasn't it
4. didn't you	10. hasn't it	16. didn't you	22. don't you
5. will he	11. didn't I	17. can't she	23. hasn't it
6. doesn't it	12. has he	18. didn't he	24. did he
7. don't they	13. did he	19. have you	25. does she

Exercise 87

2. taking	7. dancing	12. listening	17. changing
3. investing	8. coming	13. studying	18. buying
4. hitting	9. hiding	14. using	19. receiving
5. moving	10. waiting	15. painting	20. making
6. eating	11. speaking	16. opening	21. riding

Exercise 88

2. leaving	to leave	10. building	to build
3. studying	to study	11. watching	to watch
4. working	to work	12. staying	to stay
5. doing	to do	13. criticizing	to criticize
6. working	to work	14. finding	to find
7. dancing	to dance	15. speaking	to speak
8. mentioning	to mention	16. doing	to do
9. teaching	to teach	17. sending	to send

Exercise 89

2. of waiting
3. of dancing
4. on going
5. of seeing
6. about going
7. of finding
8. on speaking
9. to seeing
10. in teaching
11. in helping
12. on helping
13. of leaving
14. in learning
15. of swimming
16. in locating
17. of studying
18. of buying
19. of seeing
20. in finding
21. for managing

Exercise 90

2. bitten
3. let
4. flown
5. chose
6. worn
7. fell
8. given
9. tore
10. grew
11. hid
12. known
13. driven
14. sung
15. wrote
16. blew
17. eaten
18. found
19. led
20. lain
21. thrown
22. spread
23. froze
24. spoken

Exercise 91

2. permanently
3. board
4. telephone
5. visit
6. come for
7. prefer
8. discuss
9. examine it
10. at the point of doing
11. discard
12. up to the present
13. accustomed to
14. pretend
15. confused
16. by memory
17. be careful

Exercise 92

2. noun
   verb
3. noun
   verb
4. verb
   noun
5. noun
   verb
6. noun
   verb
7. verb
   noun
8. verb
   noun
9. verb
   noun

Exercise 93

3. weight
4. obligation
5. recognition
6. insistence
7. repetition
8. location
9. arrival
10. analysis
11. temptation
12. argument
13. adjustment
14. reaction
15. expectation
16. proof
17. description
18. arrangement
19. treatment
20. consideration
21. explanation
22. annoyance
23. appearance
24. belief
25. breath
26. confusion
27. inspection
28. admiration
29. relief
30. choice
31. embarrassment
32. destruction
33. completion
34. satisfaction
35. enjoyment
36. hesitation
37. paralysis
38. identification
39. protection
40. obedience
41. discovery
42. complaint
43. criticism
44. refusal

Exercise 94

3. to grow	15. to impress	27. to rob	39. to enter
4. to interfere	16. to marry	28. to succeed	40. to begin
5. to bury	17. to deny	29. to punish	41. to withdraw
6. to explode	18. to intend	30. to decide	42. to paralyze
7. to interrupt	19. to choose	31. to observe	43. to believe
8. to disturb	20. to approve	32. to reserve	44. to conclude
9. to apologize	21. to advise	33. to adopt	45. to refuse
10. to admit	22. to die	34. to deceive	46. to destroy
11. to repeat	23. to suspect	35. to remain	47. to criticize
12. to prove	24. to agree	36. to lose	48. to complain
13. to collect	25. to amuse	37. to fail	
14. to relieve	26. to excite	38. to warn	

Exercise 95

2. about	7. off	12. with	17. from	22. until
3. of	8. under	13. on	18. by	23. of
4. on	9. about	14. for	19. of	24. for
5. to	10. for	15. of	20. on	25. for
6. into	11. for	16. from	21. to	

Exercise 96

2. permanent	7. hairs	12. n	17. pants
3. flowed	8. brother's daughter	13. broom	18. jeweler
4. mean	9. choice	14. oars	
5. sound	10. advice	15. fare	
6. sing	11. t	16. accustomed to	

Exercise 97

2. of moving	8. is coming	14. ours	20. has worked
3. have lived	9. cries	15. sunk	21. studied
4. in learning	10. was raining	16. was	22. were watching
5. waiting	11. studying	17. could	
6. hearing	12. is supposed	18. you will	
7. painting	13. me to go	19. anywhere	

Exercise 98

2. it is	6. you are	10. I was	14. I liked	18. I put
3. I was	7. he was	11. it is	15. Adam put	19. we had
4. I would	8. she lives	12. I paid	16. she went	20. it is
5. it is	9. she lived	13. he is	17. this costs	

Exercise 99

2. ought to go
3. ought to choose
4. ought not to talk
5. ought not to write
6. ought to be
7. ought to try
8. ought to get
9. ought to have
10. ought not to speak
11. ought to obey
12. ought not to read
13. ought to write
14. ought to try
15. ought to take
16. ought to go
17. ought to be sent
18. ought to arrive
19. ought to be written
20. ought not to spend

Exercise 100

2. should have gone
3. should have arrived
4. should have gone
5. should have telephoned
6. should have been sent
7. should have been delivered
8. should have been
9. should have told
10. should have gone
11. should have been written
12. should have written
13. should have telephoned
14. should have written
15. should have spent
16. should not have wasted
17. should have been
18. should not have told
19. should have asked
20. should not have talked

Exercise 101

2. ought to have gone
3. ought to have traveled
4. ought to have saved
5. ought to have been
6. ought to have signed
7. ought to have been sent
8. ought not to have talked
9. ought to have been delivered
10. ought to have been faxed
11. ought to have seen
12. ought not to have mentioned
13. ought not to have wasted
14. ought to have explained
15. ought to have telephoned
16. ought not to have worked
17. ought to have been prepared
18. ought to have telephoned
19. ought to have gotten
20. ought to have gone
21. ought to have written
22. ought to have been put

Exercise 102

2. works
3. hurries
4. rains
5. comes
6. attend
7. is
8. telephones
9. see
10. does not
11. have
12. leave
13. gets
14. calls
15. does not
16. decide
17. gets
18. bites
19. have

Exercise 103

2. will visit
3. will miss
4. will go
5. will go
6. will learn
7. will be
8. will tell
9. will let
10. will have
11. will have
12. will be
13. will give
14. will drive
15. will take
16. will earn
17. will have
18. will explain
19. will be
20. will play

Exercise 104

2. had	5. knew	8. paid	11. liked	14. didn't have
3. owned	6. spoke	9. knew	12. had	15. didn't waste
4. worked	7. went	10. studied	13. had	16. had

Exercise 105

2. would play	7. would go	12. would walk	17. would be
3. would go	8. would get	13. would buy	18. would get
4. would speak	9. would make	14. would ask	
5. would have	10. would take	15. would give	
6. would study	11. would go	16. would stay	

Exercise 106

2. were	7. were	12. would know	17. would continue
3. were	8. were	13. would go	18. would ask
4. were	9. were	14. would go	
5. were	10. were	15. would travel	
6. were	11. would explain	16. would not be	

Exercise 107

2. had known	6. had gone	10. had thought	11. had taken
3. had telephoned	7. had told	11. had seen	15. had telephoned
4. had been	8. had received	12. had not rained	16. had known
5. had been	9. had had	13. had left	

Exercise 108

2. would have called	9. would have talked	16. would have met
3. would have gone	10. would have gotten	17. would have driven
4. would have acted	11. would have done	18. would have gone
5. would have gotten	12. would have gone	19. would have had
6. would have caught	13. would have bought	20. would have been
7. would have refused	14. would have taken	21. would have taken
8. would have given	15. would have gone	22. would have gotten

Exercise 109

2. had gone	6. had studied	10. had known	14. had	18. were
3. spoke	7. were	11. had started	15. were	19. had been
4. had	8. were	12. had studied	16. had	20. were
5. had telephoned	9. were	13. knew	17. had had	

Exercise 110

2. arrives	6. go	10. arrives	14. gets	18. comes
3. leave	7. telephone	11. get	15. telephone	19. returns
4. gets	8. get	12. gets	16. arrives	20. arrives
5. let	9. need	13. see	17. hear	

Exercise 111

3. through
4. new
5. waste
6. weigh
7. week
8. would
9. night
10. no
11. sell
12. seller
13. sent
14. seen
15. fourth
16. dye
17. flower
18. rode
19. write
20. read
21. sale
22. seas
23. birth
24. heel
25. here
26. seam
27. sum
28. whole
29. hire
30. hymn
31. meat
32. maid
33. male
34. inn
35. close
36. hour
37. brake
38. not
39. pare
40. plain
41. peace
42. by
43. roll
44. guest
45. steel
46. sow
47. sun
48. principal
49. pale
50. deer

Exercise 112

3. unable
4. unbelievable
5. irregular
6. dishonest
7. disappear
8. disobey
9. dislike
10. unattractive
11. illegible
12. mispronounce
13. disconnect
14. discontinue
15. misunderstand
16. untie
17. unwrap
18. unbutton
19. disadvantage
20. immature
21. incapable
22. disorganized
23. undress
24. unfold
25. unfortunate
26. unfair
27. disagree
28. disapprove
29. impolite
30. indiscreet
31. incorrect
32. insincere
33. uncover
34. unfurnished
35. unhealthy
36. unopened
37. unarmed
38. impatient
39. inaccurate
40. disinfect
41. disinherit
42. inconvenient
43. unreal
44. unkind
45. dissatisfied
46. disagreeable
47. unpleasant
48. independent

Exercise 113

2. to
3. in
4. with
5. in
6. by
7. of
8. up
9. for
10. to
11. to
12. on
13. for
14. with
15. on
16. in
17. in
18. from
19. since
20. from
21. on

Exercise 114

2. dull
3. arrives on time
4. width
5. paralysis
6. true
7. silent
8. partially deaf
9. taken
10. let
11. comes
12. rarely
13. lied
14. testimony
15. much
16. surrenders
17. without effective result

Exercise 115

2. I was
3. would
4. to have done
5. were
6. arrives
7. had seen
8. you live
9. theirs
10. to have been delivered
11. is ringing
12. coming
13. on waiting
14. in locating
15. is supposed
16. have you studied
17. for
18. well
19. a
20. an
21. have lived
22. comes
23. was sleeping
24. should have telephoned

Exercise 116

2. he is, too
3. I do, too
4. his brother did, too
5. she does, too
6. I will, too
7. Ed did, too
8. she has, too

9. I did, too
10. his sister was, too
11. they did, too
12. I am, too
13. he can, too
14. Ann can, to

15. she is, too
16. I do, too
17. his sister does, too
18. I will, too
19. you do, too
20. I may, too

Exercise 117

2. so will she
3. so have I
4. so do I
5. so can she
6. so did I
7. so will Gloria
8. so did my wife

9. so does her husband
10. so was his accomplice
11. so did I
12. so does her husband
13. so did we
14. so were the vegetables
15. so did my wife

16. so will Josie
17. so would I
18. so is my watch/mine
19. so is her husband
20. so did his sister

Exercise 118

2. Louise won't, either
3. she doesn't, either
4. I am/I'm not, either
5. my wife doesn't, either
6. I won't, either
7. Dick didn't, either
8. your wife won't, either
9. Molly hasn't, either

10. we didn't, either
11. he doesn't, either
12. I can't, either
13. the teacher didn't, either
14. Grace isn't, either
15. George can't, either
16. your watch/yours doesn't, either
17. Henry didn't, either

Exercise 119

2. neither did the teacher
3. neither can my wife
4. neither have I
5. neither did we
6. neither could my companion
7. neither do they
8. neither can Gail
9. neither have I
10. neither will George

11. neither did my wife
12. neither have I
13. neither is my answer/mine
14. neither do his friends
15. neither am I
16. neither did I
17. neither can Rodney
18. neither will your wife

Exercise 120

2. won't
3. didn't
4. am/I'm not
5. don't
6. do
7. didn't
8. didn't
9. will
10. haven't
11. has
12. can't
13. didn't
14. doesn't
15. do
16. doesn't
17. am
18. do
19. does
20. do

Exercise 121

3. pride
4. sickness
5. difference
6. simplicity
7. foolishness
8. youth
9. sadness
10. importance
11. difficulty
12. anger
13. depth
14. strength
15. height
16. nervousness
17. death
18. beauty
19. convenience
20. ugliness
21. gentleness
22. bitterness
23. possibility
24. width
25. sarcasm
26. ignorance
27. emphasis
28. strangeness
29. happiness
30. freedom
31. weakness
32. illness
33. sympathy
34. danger
35. dignity
36. absence
37. kindness
38. religion
39. truth
40. silence
41. intelligence
42. generosity
43. jealousy
44. cruelty
45. confidence
46. wealth
47. health
48. anxiety
49. mystery
50. noise

Exercise 122

3. advantageous
4. sarcastic
5. angry
6. fortunate
7. humorous
8. dignified
9. merciful
10. patient
11. energetic
12. dirty
13. absent
14. necessary
15. beautiful
16. disgraceful
17. rainy
18. wavy
19. affectionate
20. mysterious
21. suspicious
22. stylish
23. proud
24. sentimental
25. religious
26. ignorant
27. noisy
28. true
29. ambitious
30. powerful
31. silent
32. important
33. deep
34. high
35. wide
36. long
37. strong
38. cruel
39. intelligent
40. present
41. generous
42. bitter
43. dead
44. free
45. simple
46. confused
47. indifferent
48. regular

Exercise 123

2. to have been
3. to have had
4. to have missed
5. to have worked
6. to have met
7. to have known
8. to have known
9. to have done
10. to have seen
11. to have had
12. to have been
13. to have arrived
14. to have done
15. to have saved
16. to have known
17. to have been
18. to have liked
19. to have delivered
20. to have shown

Exercise 124

A.
2. must have come
3. must have lived
4. must have left
5. must have been
6. must have studied
7. must have been
8. must have worked

B.
2. may have delayed
3. may have lost
4. may have forgotten
5. may have stolen
6. may have taken
7. may have telephoned
8. may have been

Exercise 125

2. were
3. had had
4. will give
5. would have been killed
6. would do
7. would go
8. would have gone
9. see
10. will let
11. had had
12. studies
13. studied
14. had studied
15. would arrive
16. had seen
17. would work
18. had had
19. had not been
20. would not have happened
21. had been
22. would spend

Exercise 126

2. did not go
3. ought not to tell
4. should not have told
5. has not lived
6. were not supposed to arrive
7. cannot speak
8. will not return
9. did not have to work
10. does not have
11. is not
12. may not smoke
13. were not
14. were not driving
15. would not like
16. do not go
17. does not know
18. did not get married
19. should not lend
20. did not arrive
21. does not listen
22. will not go
23. does not smoke
24. has not been studying